Library / M...
Carroll Co...
1601 Washing...
Westminster, Maryland 21157

WITHDRAWN

D0213465

# NAPOLEON III

Library/Media Center
Carroll Community College
1601
Westminster

WITHDRAWN

# PROFILES IN POWER

*General Editor: Keith Robbins*

ELIZABETH I
## Christopher Haigh

RICHELIEU
## Robert Knecht

NAPOLEON III
## James McMillan

LLOYD GEORGE
## Martin Pugh

HITLER
## Ian Kershaw

CASTRO
## Sebastian Balfour

. . . . . . .

# NAPOLEON III

## James F. McMillan

**LONGMAN**
**London and New York**

**Longman Group UK Limited,**
Longman House, Burnt Mill, Harlow,
Essex CM20 2JE, England
*and Associated Companies throughout the world.*

*Published in the United States of America
by Longman Inc., New York*

© Longman Group UK Limited 1991

All rights reserved; no part of this publication
may be reproduced, stored in a retrieval system,
or transmitted in any form or by any means, electronic,
mechanical, photocopying, recording, or otherwise,
without either the prior written permission of the
Publishers or a licence permitting restricted copying
in the United Kingdom issued by the Copyright
Licensing Agency Ltd, 33-34 Alfred Place,
London, WC1E 7DP.

First published 1991

**British Library Cataloguing in Publication Data**
McMillan, James F. *1948–*
Napoleon III. — (Profiles in power).
I. Title
994.07092

ISBN 0-582-49483-4 PPR
ISBN 0-582-08333-2 CSD

**Library of Congress Cataloging in Publication Data**
McMillan, James F., 1948–
Napoleon III / James McMillan.
p.    cm. - (Profiles in power)
Includes bibliographical references (p.   ) and index.
ISBN 0-582-49483-4 (paper) : £6.95. - ISBN (invalid)
0-582-08333-2 (cased) : £16.95
1. Napoleon III, Emperor of the French, 1808–1873.
2. France-Kings and rulers-Biography.
3. France-History-1848-1870.
I. Title.   II. Series: Profiles in power
(London, England)
DC280.M43   1991
944.07'092-dc20
[B]

Set in 10.5/12pt Linotron 202 Baskerville

Produced by Longman Singapore Publishers (Pte) Ltd.
Printed in Singapore

# CONTENTS

# LIST OF MAPS

For Donatella, my Wife

*Chapter 1*

# NAPOLEON III AND
# THE HISTORIANS

What posterity would make of him was something which mattered a great deal to Napoleon III. Historians, however, have disagreed as much as contemporaries over his character, aims and achievements. His admirers usually portray him as the unfortunate victim of a long tradition of historiographical vilification, but the fact is that he has had a good press for over half a century, especially in Britain and America. He may still await his French national monument (would-be pilgrims must visit his tomb at Farnborough Abbey, Hampshire) but the 'black legend' that once attached to his regime has been dispelled by historical scholarship.[1]

The basic explanation for the wide divergence of opinion is that, well into the twentieth century, the writing of history continued to be a highly partisan activity in France, both reflecting and reinforcing the ideological divisions created by the Revolution and the revolutionary tradition. From a republican perspective, Napoleon III was not only the ignominious failure who had led France to shameful defeat in the Franco-Prussian War but also the man of blood, the usurper who on 2 December 1851 violently overthrew the Second Republic.[2] The fact that prominent writers and artists with republican sympathies were among the fiercest critics of the regime also helped to damage his reputation with posterity. Victor Hugo pilloried the Emperor as a 'bandit' and dubbed him 'Napoleon the Little'.[3] The painter and satirist Daumier invented the character 'Ratapoil', a louche, cynical and self-seeking adventurer, to epitomise the Empire.[4] Out of the same historiographical stable came Taxil de Lord's *Histoire du Second Empire* (six volumes 1867–75), a rambling and abusive work by an opposition journalist and future republican deputy.

I

Not even the 'professionalisation' of history in France rescued Napoleon from his detractors, since the leading lights of the profession were rarely free of a marked republican bias. Under the Third Republic the academy served the state and the historian was expected to defend the regime and its ideals. Thus for Lavisse and Seignobos, Protestants and anticlericals both as well as successive holders of the prestigious chair of History at the Sorbonne, the Empire had to be judged by its origins and early authoritarian character, though Seignobos did distinguish the Emperor from his regime, portraying him as a not unsympathetic but administratively incompetent figure, a prey to his venal and cynical Orleanist advisers.[5]

The distinction between the Emperor and the Empire was also drawn by historians who studied from other political vantage points. Albert Thomas, from a reformist socialist perspective, noted Napoleon III's idealism and sincerity, but characterised the Empire as a reactionary regime founded on the Emperor's personal ambitions. As a socialist Thomas was particularly interested in how the workers had fared under the Empire. His verdict was that they were ill-served by the regime's paternalistic social policies and that the development of their organisation was hampered by the controls imposed by an authoritarian bureaucratic state. Nevertheless, he argued, by 1870 there were clear signs that the workers had become the advance guard of a mounting republican challenge to the regime. For a republican socialist like Thomas it was important to deny that the Second Empire had any genuine popular roots, particularly among workers.[6]

From a very different ideological standpoint, namely that of a Catholic and a conservative, Pierre de la Gorce was ready to concede that Napoleon III possessed many admirable traits, but he deplored the consequences of the advent of the Empire (not least the marginalisation of the former Orleanist establishment). The trouble with the Emperor, according to La Gorce, was that he was a visionary and a Utopian and, worse, an intriguer and adventurer. At once dreamer and conspirator, he launched France on the road to Sedan, the shameful evidence of a national decadence the origins of which went back to the Revolution. On the other hand, La Gorce acknowledged that Napoleon III was genuinely committed to the liberalisation of the Empire. The establishment of the Liberal Empire therefore represented an achievement, even if its effectiveness was blunted through the influence of hardline authoritarian Bonapartists like Rouher. (La Gorce shared the view of Seignobos that Napoleon III was not completely master in his own house).[7] Indeed, in a later evaluation, written just before his death, La Gorce felt that he might have judged the Emperor too harshly in his multi-volume work and portrayed him as a man 'so good and even enlightened', more of a humanitarian philosopher than a states-man, always well-meaning, but hopelessly inadequate for the business of statecraft, and in the end destroyed by forces which he had unwittingly helped to unleash.[8]

A still greater apologist for the Liberal Empire was its former chief minister Emile Ollivier. His seventeen-volume *Empire libéral*, published between 1895 and 1918, was both a history of the regime and an exhaustive defence of his stewardship. Ollivier represented Napoleon III as a far-sighted and progress-ive leader and himself as his dedicated servant in the great work of reconciling liberalism, democracy and the principle of order. An old '48er', Ollivier claimed that the Emperor too remained at heart a man of that era and always intended to crown the edifice of the Empire with the restoration of liberty. For that reason, and because the Empire combined material prosperity at home with the pursuit of a generous and glorious policy abroad, he had been able to rally to the regime. The tragedy of the Liberal Empire was that the great experiment had been cut short not through any shortcomings on the part of Napoleon III or his minister but by the machinations of Bismarck and irresponsible political opponents in France (Thiers above all) who stirred up the dangerous anti-Prussian sentiments which left the government few options in the diplomatic crisis of 1870.[9]

In France the works of La Gorce and Ollivier failed to dent the negative view of Napoleon III which held sway at the Sorbonne, but in Britain and America they contributed to the elaboration of a positive, sometimes flattering, view of the Emperor. In the Anglo-Saxon world he has enjoyed favourable treatment since the publication of Blanchard Jerrold's authorised biography which drew on documentation made available by the Bonaparte family,[10] though the crucial volumes for the aca-demic community were those of the Cambridge historian F A Simpson.[11] In his estimation the Second Empire was a much more important episode in European history than the First and its ruler was the man who, more than any other individual, shattered the status quo of the Vienna settlement, leaving 'both

3

the map and the moral order of Europe revolutionised'.[12] For Simpson Napoleon III not only restored (temporarily) French preponderance in Europe but also championed 'the struggling and unorthodox cause of nationality' in such a way as to promote 'its unexpected triumph'.[13] Simpson did retain certain reservations about flaws in the character of Louis Napoleon, but some of his successors were unstinting in their eulogies. For Robert Sencourt, he was 'the modern emperor', a man of the twentieth century, out of joint with his own times but someone who would have rejoiced to live in a world which had given birth to the League of Nations.[14] Albert Guérard, a French expatriate who made his career teaching in the USA, extolled 'the unfailing gentleness, the quiet intellectual courage, the profound generosity of Napoleon III'.[15]

It is true that Napoleon III has had his British and American critics. Whig historians such as H A L Fisher and G P Gooch, sympathetic to nineteenth-century liberalism, were critical of the authoritarian aspects of Bonapartism.[16] Later, writing in a world which had experienced the horrors of totalitarian dictatorship, a number of historians looked back and discovered in Napoleon III a precursor of Mussolini and Hitler. Sir Lewis Namier dismissed him as 'the first mountebank dictator'.[17] The predominant view, however, continues to be favourable, even if sympathetic biographers tediously insist on their mission to rescue the French emperor from the slanders of the 'black legend'.[18]

In France, too, more favourable appraisals have emerged, after the French academic establishment began to shift its preoccupations towards social and economic history.[19] The Second Empire's commitment to economic expansion and to the alleviation of some of the miseries engendered by industrialisation allow it to be seen as an essentially 'modern' regime. In this light, Napoleon III appears as a technocratic visionary, a 'Saint-Simon on horseback'. The most recent French work is free from the abuse which Anglo-Saxon authors too readily attribute to Gallic historians of the Empire.[20] In reality, a historiography which privileges the 'black legend' is out of date by some forty years.

What remains central to any reassessment is the question of power. The present volume tries to establish the importance of the personal factor in the evolution of a personalist regime. Napoleon was in office continuously for twenty-one years. How did he manage to retain power? How free was he to take the political initiative both at home and abroad? What did he achieve? The history of the Second Empire and the biography of Napoleon III are not one and the same. Obviously, they interacted. The problem is to discover what *difference* Napoleon III made to his times.

. . . . .

## NOTES AND REFERENCES

1. An excellent introduction to the historiography is Campbell S L 1978 *The Second Empire Revisited: a Study in French Historiography*. Rutgers. Also useful are Spitzer A B 1962 'The good Napoleon III', *French Historical Studies* 2 (Spring), pp. 308–29, and Spencer W F 1976 'New images of Napoleon III: foreign policy', *Proceedings of the Western Society for French History* Denver, CO, ed. Gooch B D. The *Revue d'Histoire Moderne et Contemporaine* XXI (Jan–March 1974) devotes the whole issue to the historiography of the Second Empire

2. Cf. Arnaud R 1939 *The Second Republic and Napoleon III* (trans. E F Buckley). Heinemann; Hanotaux G 1929 *Histoire de la nation française*

3. Hugo V 1853 *Les châtiments*; 1877 *Histoire d'un crime* 2 vols; 1853 *Napoléon le petit*

4. On Daumier, see Clark T J 1973 *The Absolute Bourgeois: Artists and Politics in France 1848–1851*. Thames & Hudson

5. Seignobos C 1921 *Histoire de la France contemporaine* ed Lavisse E, vol 6 *La Révolution de 1848 – Le Second Empire* and vol 7 *Le déclin de l'empire et l'établissement de la Troisième République*. On the latter see Nora P 1962 'Ernest Lavisse: son rôle dans la formation du sentiment national', *Revue Historique* 228, pp. 73–106

6. *Thomas A 1907 Histoire socialiste* vol 10, ed. J. Jaurès *Le second Empire*

7. Gorce P de la 1921 (1894–1904) *Histoire du second Empire*. 7 vols

8. Gorce P de la 1933 *Napoléon III et sa politique*

9. Ollivier E 1895–1918 *L' Empire libéral: études, récits, souvenirs*. 17 vols and 1 table

10. Jerrold B 1874–82 *The Life of Napoleon III*, 4 vols, Longman

11. Simpson F A 1951 (3rd edn; 1st edn 1909) *The Rise of Louis*

*Napoleon.* Longman; Simpson F A 1960 (3rd edn; 1st edn 1923) *Louis Napoleon and the Recovery of France.* Longman

12. Simpson 1960 (3rd edn), Preface
13. Ibid.
14. Sencourt R 1933 *The Modern Emperor.* Appleton–Century
15. Guérard A 1943 *Napoleon III.* Harvard University Press, p. 293
16. Fisher H A L 1914 *Bonapartism.* Oxford University Press; Gooch G P 1960 *The Second Empire.* Longman
17. Namier L 1963 'The first mountebank dictator' in *Vanished Supremacies*, Harper, pp. 54–64; Schapiro J S 1949 *Liberalism and the Challenge of Fascism.* McGraw-Hill, pp. 320–31
18. Cf. Corley T A B 1961 *Democratic Despot: a Life of Napoleon III.* Barrie & Rockliff; Smith W H C 1972 *Napoleon III*, Wayland, and his more recent French version, *Napoléon III* (1982)
19. The key work was Blanchard M 1950 *Le Second Empire*
20. Most recently Plessis A 1985 (French edn, 1979) *The Rise and Fall of the Second Empire 1852–1871.* Cambridge University Press; and Girard L 1986 *Napoléon III*

# Chapter 2

# PREPARING FOR POWER

Controversy over Napoleon III extends even to the circumstances of his birth. Charles Louis Napoleon Bonaparte was born in Paris on 20 April 1808, ostensibly the son of Hortense Beauharnais and Louis Bonaparte, brother of the Emperor Napoleon and of the King of Holland. But, since the marriage with Hortense was not a happy one, doubts have lingered regarding Louis's paternity. The youthful Hortense, daughter of the Empress Joséphine by her first marriage, was bright and extrovert, her husband morose and neurotic, possibly a repressed homosexual. Their unlikely union, consecrated on 4 January 1802 by Cardinal Caprara, the Papal Legate, owed its origins to the limitless dynastic ambitions of Napoleon I. Despite the birth in rapid succession of two children (Napoleon-Charles, on 10 October 1802, and Napoleon-Louis, on 11 October 1804) the couple began to spend more and more time apart. Hortense certainly had lovers, and in 1811 was to give birth to an illegitimate son, fathered by the comte de Flahaut (himself the illegitimate son of Talleyrand) who would later be famous as the duc de Morny. Nevertheless, even if accusations that Louis Napoleon was not really a Bonaparte cannot be refuted definitively, most biographers are agreed that he was in all probability the son of Louis, conceived during a brief reconciliation with Hortense following the sudden death of their first-born child in May 1807.[1]

The reunion was shortlived. Only the veto of the Emperor, preoccupied with his own divorce from Joséphine, prevented a split in 1808. But in 1810 Louis abdicated, fleeing to Bohemia and leaving Hortense to return to Paris from Holland with her two boys. Napoleon himself took a keen interest in their upbringing. Young Louis Napoleon was baptised at Fontainebleau in 1810 with the Emperor and his new Empress, Marie-Louise of Austria, as godparents. As the first prince to be born since the proclamation of the Empire, he had a special place in his uncle's affections and Hortense and her children were regular guests at the Tuileries when Napoleon was in residence. The boy was also spoiled by his grandmother Joséphine, now styled the 'Dowager Empress', and living in splendour in the Château of Malmaison. Louis Napoleon grew up a likeable and affectionate but timid and sensitive child, adoring his indulgent mother, but perhaps suffering from the lack of a father.

The boy's personality and development owned as much to the turn of French national politics as to his family background. The collapse of the Empire inevitably had consequences for Hortense and her sons, especially after her enthusiastic support for Napoleon during the One Hundred Days Campaign cost her the favour of Tsar Alexander I, whom she had charmed in 1814 when the Emperor first abdicated. Expelled from France and deprived of legal custody of her elder child, now reclaimed by his father, Hortense and Louis Napoleon began a long experience of exile, moving restlessly between Bavaria and Switzerland before settling definitively at Arenenberg by Lake Constance. Their wanderings among the romantic scenery may well have stirred the boy's imagination and sensibilities, but they were bad for his formal education, all the more so in that his tutor, the amiable but idle abbé Bertrand, made few efforts to curb his natural laziness. Only in 1820, with the engagement of the more austere and demanding Philippe Le Bas, son of a Jacobin and regicide, was Louis Napoleon introduced to the notion of a timetable. Le Bas remained the boy's tutor until 1828 and succeeded in imparting some of his own scholarly tastes. Even so, as Le Bas endlessly complained, Hortense's ceaseless travels continued to interrupt his studies, though they did expose him to the heady delights of Italy, with not inconsiderable consequences for the future.

At Arenenberg Louis Napoleon was steeped in reminders of the First Empire. Hortense reared him on the lore of past glories and turned the house into a Napoleonic shrine. Their drawing-room replicated that of Malmaison. Other Bonapartes and Beauharnais joined them – Hortense's brother Eugène, Jérôme, former King of Westphalia – along with veteran officers of the *grande armée*. But, however much the exiles' nostalgic talk may have made the youthful Louis Napoleon yearn for an

8

imperial restoration, it is unlikely that at this time he ever envisaged himself as Emperor. The pretender was Napoleon's son by Marie-Louise, the duc de Reichstadt, who lived in Vienna, a virtual prisoner at the palace of Schönbrunn, while his elder brother Napoleon-Louis, brought up by his father ex-King Louis in Florence, also took precedence over him, as did his uncles. Later, Louis Napoleon would talk a great deal about his faith in his destiny, but in 1830 he seemed to have no future beyond part-time soldiering in the Swiss army, in which he had enrolled as a volunteer. Not even the exciting news from Paris relating the overthrow of Charles X and his replacement by the 'Citizen King' Louis Philippe in July 1830 held out the prospect of change, for the new monarch was no more disposed than his predecessors to re-admit the Bonapartes to France. Louis Napoleon's destiny in the autumn of 1830 seemed to be to live a life of aimless, if comfortable, exile.

It was at this point that, not for the last time, events in Italy had a decisive impact on his fortunes. Having gone south for the winter, as was their habit, Louis Napoleon and Hortense found themselves in Rome at a moment when revolution had broken out in various parts of Italy, including the Papal States, then arguably the worst governed territories in Europe. Louis Napoleon sympathised with the insurgents but refused to join, let alone lead, a hopeless rising planned for 11 December. Nevertheless, taking no chances, the authorities ordered his expulsion from the Papal States. On retreating to Florence, however, he discovered that his elder brother was even more susceptible to the Italian revolutionary cause, having in all probability become a member of the secret society the Carbonari. It seems unlikely that Louis Napoleon himself ever swore the Carbonarist oath, but both brothers responded enthusiastically when on January 1831 they were invited to enlist with the revolutionaries. Each was placed in charge of a detachment of troops and Louis Napoleon rejoiced at his first taste of military action. As he wrote from Terni: 'For the first time I know what it is to live; up to now I have done nothing but vegetate.'[2]

His exhilaration was short-lived. As Metternich's Austria moved to crush the rebels, the Italian patriots realised that only French assistance could save them: and no French help would be forthcoming from Louis Philippe while Bonaparte princes were active in the Italian cause. The revolutionaries recalled the brothers from the battlefield to Bologna. Sentenced to death by the Austrians and compelled to flee before their advancing troops, they reached Forlì, where Napoleon Louis was stricken with measles and died on 11 March. Louis Napoleon was also infected and might also have died but for the timely arrival of Hortense, who supervised his recovery and escape in a manner worthy of the best traditions of romantic fiction. At one stage he was hospitalised at Ancona in a room adjacent to that of the Austrian commander. Eventually, disguised as a footman and then as an Englishman, he and his resourceful mother reached Paris, where Hortense threw herself on the clemency of Louis Philippe. The King was gracious, but adamant that there was still no place in France for the Bonapartes. Louis Napoleon's ill health meant that mother and son were able to delay their departure until after they had witnessed from their hotel window the crowds who swarmed into the place Vendôme on 5 May 1831 (the tenth anniversary of the Emperor's death) to celebrate around the Vendôme column. The following day they made for Calais and from there sailed to London, where they stayed three months, enjoying the status of celebrities.

Back in Switzerland Louis Napoleon began to take stock of all his recent experiences. From 1831 he was convinced that Bonapartist sentiment was still strong among the ordinary people of France and in the French army, and that his mission in life should be to work for an imperial restoration. In London, for the first time, he became a Bonapartist conspirator, responding positively to the overtures of an adventurer of Scottish descent known as Count Lennox who, through the agency of his wife, suggested that the prince should finance Bonapartist propaganda in France and collaborate with other revolutionary organisations bent on the overthrow of the July Monarchy. Louis Philippe's government discovered the plot, arrested Lennox but, not wishing to boost publicity for the Bonapartists, attempted to hush up the affair.[3] The death of his brother was also of crucial importance. In addition to being a personal tragedy, it stirred in Louis Napoleon the notion that it was he personally who would have to lead the Bonapartist crusade, in the first instance on behalf of 'Napoleon II', the duc de Reichstadt, but ultimately on his own behalf, since the son of Napoleon and Marie-Louise was sick with consumption at Schönbrunn, and neither his father nor his uncle Joseph, the Emperor's brothers, had given any indication of wishing to head a Bonapartist challenge. The death of the duc de Reichstadt in July 1832 consolidated his belief in his own destiny. From 1832 Louis Napoleon's life was spent in preparation for the day when he would exercise power as Emperor of the French.

As a first step, he began to produce propaganda to bring his name to the attention of the public. His earliest exercise in self-advertisement was *Rêveries politiques*, published in May 1832. Written while 'Napoleon II' was still alive but seriously ill, it may or may not be a statement about his personal ambitions. In essence, it called for a marriage between Bonapartism and republicanism, and included the outline of a future constitution which recognised the principle of popular sovereignty but reserved for the Emperor the right to execute the people's will, with deputies elected only by indirect suffrage. More substantial was the *Considérations politiques et militaires sur la Suisse* which followed in 1833, a work ostensibly analysing the Swiss system of government and well received in his adopted country, but which really set out to remind the French of what the First Empire had stood for; namely, stability, liberty and independence. Here were themes that Louis Napoleon would later develop at greater length in *Des idées napoléoniennes*. As a Bonaparte, he was also keen to reveal himself an authority on military matters. In 1836 he published a military handbook entitled *Manuel d'artillerie*, though for the time being it seemed that any reputation he might gain as a soldier would have to be in the rank of captain in the Swiss army.

In 1836 Louis Napoleon's prospects did not appear bright. In his personal life it was because he appeared to have no future that a projected marriage between himself and his cousin Mathilde fell through. On the political front, more dramatic means than pamphleteering seemed to be required to advance his claims to the imperial throne. Encouraged by a new acquaintance, the self-styled vicomte de Persigny, an ex-royalist and ex-republican turned fanatical Bonapartist, the pretender decided to attempt a coup.

The idea was not as madcap as it is sometimes made out to be. The July Monarchy lacked popular roots. A certain amount of support for the Empire had been expressed in 1830, during the Revolution. While a fugitive in Paris in 1831 Louis Napoleon had witnessed the demonstrations in favour of the Empire at the place Vendôme on the occasion of the tenth anniversary of

Napoleon I's death. As we shall see, a 'Napoleonic legend' was growing.[4] Strasbourg, the place selected to launch the coup, was a sensible choice. Many of its citizens were opponents of the July Monarchy and a number of junior officers in its garrison were known to be Bonapartist sympathisers. In the event, however, the coup turned into a fiasco, foiled by the commander of the garrison, who rallied his troops by denouncing Louis Napoleon as an imposter. Begun at 5 a.m. on 30 October 1836, the attempted *putsch* was over three hours later. The government, keen to minimise the Bonapartist challenge, refused to make a martyr of the prince and expelled him to the USA. Nevertheless, the regime had received a nasty shock, and Louis Napoleon was heartened by the encouraging reception he had had among a number of the soldiers. In any case, the most important thing was to have established his claim to be recognised as the Bonapartist heir-apparent. In that sense, Strasbourg was far from a failure.

More convinced than ever that his day would come eventually, he did not linger long in America. News that his mother was seriously ill brought him back first to England and thence to Switzerland. He arrived at Arenenberg on 4 August 1838, but Hortense lasted only until 5 October. The French government granted her dying wish to be buried at Malmaison, but Louis Napoleon was refused permission to attend. On the contrary, irked by his return from the New World, and provoked further by publication of an account of the Strasbourg affair by Lieutenant Laity, one of the prince's fellow conspirators, the French authorities put diplomatic pressure on Switzerland to expel him. Such treatment merely served to make Louis Napoleon known to a wider public. One newspaper regretted that, from being seen as a madman, he was being turned into a hero.[5] Another noted that he was no longer a Swiss citizen, but 'Napoleon III', the new pretender.[6] Revelling in all the publicity, Louis Napoleon retreated to London in October 1838 and once more enjoyed being lionised by high society.[7]

The demands of social life did not prevent him from pursuing his political ambitions. Most of his time was spent in a private room at the British Museum at work on a pamphlet which was published in the summer of 1839 under the title *Des idées napoléoniennes*. It was his political manifesto and an immediate success, being three times reprinted in the space of a few months and translated into six languages. Aligning himself with the world which had emerged from the French Revolution and affirming his belief in progress, Louis Napoleon argued that government must be 'the beneficent motive power of all social organisation' and that the best form of government would be that which employed 'the necessary means to open a smooth and easy road for advancing civilisation'. The problem with the Revolution was that, in pursuit of its laudable goals, it had given rise to conflict and chaos which had threatened to tear the nation asunder. Fortunately for France, as at other epochs, a saviour of society had appeared in the shape of a great man. Napoleon, the latter-day Alexander, Caesar and Charlemagne, had undertaken to reconcile the Revolution with the *ancien régime* and succeeded in restoring order and national unity. His ultimate objectives had been liberty and European peace, but his goals had not been attained because of the implacable enmity of England, which failed to appreciate that what the Emperor wanted was a European confederation based upon the principle of nationalities and of 'general interests fairly satisfied'. The programme of the Emperor retained its relevance in the France of Louis Philippe and the Europe of Metternich. The Napoleonic idea awaited fulfilment but, it was implied, at least it had an heir to whom the French people could turn.

Louis Napoleon now had a doctrine but he still lacked a party. Much of the very considerable fortune which he had inherited from his mother was spent trying to build one. He subsidised a number of newspapers and various clubs in the hope of widening his appeal. In Paris Persigny had published a brochure *Lettre de Londres, visite à prince Louis en 1840*, which suggested that the Pretender would be ready when the call came. Bonapartist agents continued to try to seduce the military in parts of the north and east of France. These propaganda efforts were all a prelude to a second attempt at a coup. The moment again was not ill-chosen. In 1840 the government's policy was under fire from the parliamentary opposition regarding events in the Near East. In addition, the return of the Emperor's body from St Helena persuaded Louis Napoleon that a Bonaparte rather than the July Monarchy could be the ultimate beneficiary of the Napoleonic legend.

The second *putsch* was launched from London, and involved the same basic strategy as had been adopted at Strasbourg; namely, to win over the military and then march on Paris, raising popular support en route. On 6 August Louis Napoleon and a party of fifty-odd fellow conspirators reached Boulogne after a rough Channel crossing aboard the paddle-steamer *The Edinburgh Castle*. Chained to the ship's mast was a tame vulture, substituting for the imperial eagle. The comic opera element was present from the start, and the expedition quickly degenerated into a débâcle even more complete than that of Strasbourg. The officers of the Boulogne garrison rallied their troops, and Louis Napoleon and his motley crew were forced to fall back to the sea. The Prince was wounded while trying to return to *The Edinburgh Castle* in a small boat, and had to be rescued from the waves. The *Punch* cartoon which depicted Louis being fished out of the water on a boat hook was a not inaccurate depiction of the whole sorry episode.

Boulogne may have been another fiasco but this time the government decided that it could not go unpunished. Instead of bringing the case before a local court, which after Strasbourg had resulted in the acquittal of the conspirators, the authorities decided to make Louis Napoleon stand trial before the Chamber of Peers. This, however, gave the Pretender another opportunity to publicise his case. In a stirring speech he told his accusers that he represented a principle, a cause and a defeat:

> The principle is the sovereignty of the people: the cause is that of the Empire; the defeat is Waterloo. You have acknowledged the principle: you have served the cause: as for the defeat, it is for you to avenge it.[8]

Louis and his lawyer maître Berryer (who as a legitimist had his own reasons for wishing to challenge the authority of the Orleanist dynasty) succeeded in embarrassing the judges. Did not many of them owe their rank to the Empire, and so how then should they presume to condemn Louis Napoleon for advocating Bonapartism? Was it right to resurrect the dead emperor from his tomb while trying to bury the living hope of his line? The verdict, however, was never in doubt. Louis Napoleon was found guilty and sentenced to imprisonment in perpetuity. He accepted the judgement stoically, asking only: how long is perpetuity?

The answer in his case proved to be six years. During that time his home was the dreary fortress of Ham in Picardy. Imprisonment had its uses. Boulogne, like Strasbourg, had not been a complete disaster, since it presented Louis and his supporters with an opportunity to make propaganda out of his status as a victim of state repression – a figure with whom a popular audience would have no difficulty in identifying. It was through imprisonment, too, that he regained the national soil. Prison life was hardly pleasant, and probably did long-term damage to his health, but the regime could have been worse. He was not incarcerated in the medieval dungeon but given two rooms to himself. For company, he had his fellow conspirators General Montholon and Dr Conneau, along with the services of his faithful valet Thélin, who chose to follow him to prison. Nor was sexual deprivation one of his problems, since he was allowed to receive visitors and succeeded in fathering two children by a local seamstress who worked in the prison. Reading and correspondence kept his mind occupied – he would later describe Ham as his 'university'. He began but never finished a *Life of Charlemagne* and composed *Fragments historiques 1688 et 1830*, in which he drew a parallel between the fate of the Stuarts, victims of their reliance upon a faction and on a foreign power, and the situation of the July Monarchy. Whereas Guizot liked to think of the Bourbons as the French Stuarts and Louis Philippe as William of Orange, Louis Napoleon suggested that it was the Orleanist regime which was destined to suffer the end of the Stuarts, while he himself would emerge in the role of William III. He concluded with a moral which he made his watchword: 'March at the head of your century, and its ideas will follow and support you. March behind them, and they will drag you along. March against them, and they will overthrow you.'[9]

Louis Napoleon was determined to march at the head of the ideas of his time. He kept up with contemporary political events and contributed articles to local newspapers. He wrote also on military matters and on the sugar-beet industry, and drew up plans for cutting a canal across Nicaragua. His principal correspondent and research assistant was Hortense Cornu, daughter of his mother's maid and his former childhood companion. An uncompromising republican, she may well have helped him develop his ideas in a more radical direction.[10] Other pastimes included conducting chemistry experiments and gardening.

The most substantial product of Louis Napoleon's prison years was *The Extinction of Poverty*, published in 1844. At a time when the 'social question', the plight of the workers in industrial society, was the subject of a profusion of comment by concerned contemporaries, Louis Napoleon made his own contribution to the debate by advocating agricultural colonies as a possible solution to the problems of unemployment and starvation wages. Having criticised the liberal economic system for its failure to capitalise upon the full productive capacity of the community and its engendering of needless misery and threats to social order, he proposed that the state should make funds available to associations of workers to permit them to take over huge tracts of uncultivated wasteland, where they could establish camps which would at first be organised in conformity with military discipline. The workers would elect leaders from their own ranks who would be responsible to the Ministry of the Interior. Work would allow the indigent to acquire property and at the same time boost the productivity of the economy. Workers who remained in the cities would also receive higher wages because none would wish to leave the colonies if wages elsewhere remained low. *L'Extinction du paupérisme* was not specially original, and combined strands from the works of Utopian thinkers of the time such as Saint-Simon, Fourier, Cabet and Louis Blanc (the latter was one of his visitors at Ham, and Hortense Cornu enrolled him as a subscriber to the workers' newspaper *L'Atelier*). It cannot be classified as 'socialist' in inspiration, but was rather a reflection of its author's views on the need for military-style leadership and vigorous state intervention. Its solution to the problem of poverty was no more (or less) ludicrous than those of other Utopian writers and hardly calculated to appeal to workers themselves. What the pamphlet did, however, was to establish Louis Napoleon's reputation as a friend of the worker. Six editions appeared between 1844 and 1848, and they certainly did him no harm in the working-class *quartiers* of the capital in the presidential elections of 1848.

Literary production, study, receiving visitors and regular sex were not enough to reconcile Louis Napoleon to his prison regime. By 1845 his spirits were at a low ebb and his mind had begun to turn increasingly to thoughts of escape. The opportunity came in 1846, while some repairs were being carried out in the prison. In the guise of a workman Louis coolly walked away carrying a plank. Within twelve hours he had reached London by way of Belgium. He soon resumed his contacts with fashionable society and the *demi-monde*, acquiring a succession of mistresses who included the famous French actress Rachel and, most notoriously, the English courtesan Miss Howard. But in the midst of his pleasures he never forgot that he was the Imperial Pretender to the throne of France. Sympathetic English acquaintances were either amused or astonished to hear him refer to the projects he would carry out 'when I become Emperor.'[11] No pretender ever had greater faith in his destiny. And events in France soon justified his confidence.

. . .

## NOTES AND REFERENCES

1. Dansette A 1961 *Louis Napoléon à la conquête du pouvoir* has an extensive discussion of the circumstances of Louis Napoleon's birth
2. Simpson F A 1951 (3rd edn; 1st edn 1909) *The Rise of Louis Napoleon*, Longman p. 67
3. The importance of the Lennox affair is suggested by Bluche F 1980 *Le Bonapartisme 1800–1850*, p. 210
4. See Chapter 3 below
5. Dansette 1961, p. 153
6. Guest I 1952 *Napoléon III in England*. British Technical & General Press, p. 31
7. Ibid.
8. Quoted by Simpson 1951, p. 141
9. *Oeuvres de Napoléon III* I, p. 342
10. Emerit M 1937 *Madame Cornu et Napoléon III*
11. Guest 1952

# THE ROAD TO POWER

From his upbringing and personal experience, Louis Napoleon had come to see himself as the heir of the first Napoleon, the man destined to restore the Bonapartes to their rightful place as rulers of France. That his private fantasies came to be realised owed little to his own impact on the French political scene before 1848 and a great deal to the inability of either the Bourbon Restoration or the July Monarchy to establish constitutional monarchy as a form of government capable of generating consensus politics. He was also powerfully assisted by the survival of a genuine popular Bonapartism quite distinct from the cult of Napoleon which developed rapidly among many sections of French opinion after Napoleon's defeat and exile. A quite separate attachment to the cause of the Empire itself among peasants and workers never entirely disappeared, and Louis Napoleon would owe much of his success in 1848 to his ability to present himself as a 'Napoleon of the people'.[1]

·  ·  ·

## THE FAILURE OF CONSTITUTIONAL
## MONARCHY

Louis Napoleon was born into a world dominated by his uncle, the Emperor Napoleon, then at the height of his power. By the time he was six, that world had been shattered. In 1814, in the aftermath of military reverses, he was forced to abdicate, and the Bourbons in the corpulent person of Louis XVIII, returned to the throne of France. The new regime inspired little enthusiasm, but after twenty-five long years of revolution, counter-revolution and warfare, the French were ready for peace. The fallen Emperor, unreconciled to defeat and knowing that he still commanded the loyalty of many ordinary people and of former soldiers, made one last desperate bid for power in the One Hundred Days campaign, which ended in his defeat at Waterloo on 18 June 1815. The Restoration was consolidated, but not before the return of Napoleon had revealed France to be a deeply divided nation, ideologically split by the legacy of the Revolution and the Empire.

Around the deposed Emperor there grew up both a myth and a legend. In 1815 the myth already existed, having been created by Napoleon himself. It portrayed him as a military genius, all-powerful conqueror and masterful ruler of a world empire. After 1815 he added another element, that of the chained Prometheus of St Helena. The legend incorporated the myth but was fostered essentially by veterans of the *grande armée*, who developed other themes, such as the cult of the army, nostalgia for military glory and a second coming of the Emperor. Under the Constitutional Monarchy, the legend grew steadily, diffused by poets such as Delavigne and Hugo, song-writers like Béranger, lithographers, painters, and the purveyors of popular literature. Historians such as Thiers also played their part. The growth of the Napoleonic legend did not necessarily produce Bonapartist politics, but it did nothing to discourage Louis Napoleon from believing that he was destined to be its principal beneficiary.[2]

He was all the more entitled to his belief in that Bonapartism remained a significant, if minority, force in popular politics. This popular Bonapartism expressed hatred of France's ruling dynasty and hopes for a re-establishment of the Empire. At first, aspirations centred on a messianic return on the part of Napoleon himself, on the model of the escape from Elba. Even after 1821, there were peasants who refused to believe that he was dead. It was also known that he had an heir, and the cause of 'Napoleon II', encouraged by secret societies like the Carbonari, could give rise to popular demonstrations in the 1820s. Those arrested for expressing their loyalty to the Empire included rural and urban artisans (notably from the clothing industry) as well as small cultivators and rural day labourers (the latter notorious for their dissemination of rumours on their frequent travels in search of work). Commercial travellers and hawkers were likewise another source of false information, while support for the Bonapartist cause remained widespread in the army. Geographically, popular Bonapartism was strongest in the departments of eastern France and in certain enclaves of the ultra-royalist bastions of the west and south-west, where the Bonapartist minority refused to yield to its persecutors. For 'Jacobin' Bonapartists like those of Lorraine, Alsace and the Franche-Comté, the Bourbons were hated both as the symbols of defeat in war and as the representatives of a hated feudal order. Even if there was no clear ideology evident in the popular Bonapartism of the Restoration period, it existed in an inchoate, sentimental and oral form which expressed revulsion for the Bourbon state. True, the Revolution of 1830 was a setback to popular Bonapartism, given the failure to revive the Empire under 'Napoleon II'. Nevertheless, Louis Napoleon was not deluded in his conviction that his name evoked memories and resonances in the minds of many ordinary people, and that the cult of the late Emperor could ultimately be fused with a Bonapartism of the people in a manner that would bring him to power. That, after all, is what happened at the end of 1848.

Not that the failure of the Bourbons was a foregone conclusion. Its critics made much of the narrow base of the franchise, under which only wealthy men paying 300 francs a year in taxation were allowed to vote, but for its day the Charter was an advanced constitution. Parliamentary debate attained high standards and the regime provided a climate in which it was possible for political liberalism to develop. In particular a liberal press emerged in the shape of newspapers such as *Le Journal des Débats* and *Le National*. In Louis XVIII the Restoration had a monarch who, though at heart a man of the eighteenth century, realistically appreciated that there could be no return to the *ancien régime*. Through his capable ministers he pursued the delicate work of national reconciliation, refusing to bow to pressure from royalist diehards (the Ultras) who wanted to see a full-scale counter-revolution. (In 1816 he dissolved the Ultra-dominated Chamber of Deputies to obtain a more moderate parliamentary majority.)

The misfortune of the Restoration was that in the end the Ultras gained the upper hand. Even before Louis XVIII's death he had been forced to make concessions to their power. After the One Hundred Days, reprisals against Napoleon's supporters were carried out in a massive purge of the administration and in a series of show trials. In the Midi, beyond the monarch's control, an unofficial 'white terror' was unleashed against Bonapartists, republicans and – in the case of the department of the Gard – Protestants. Again, after the assassination in 1820 of the duc de Berry, son of the count of Artois, the King's brother and chief Ultra, the influence of the reactionaries grew. When, in 1824, Artois succeeded the childless Louis XVIII, reaction intensified to the point where, six years later, France seemed to be heading back to the old order. Former *émigrés* were voted an indemnity. A law introduced the death penalty for sacrilege. In 1830 the King's determination to impose a reactionary ministry unable to command a parliamentary majority, along with his efforts to annul the results of recent elections, reduce the size of the electorate and curb freedom of the press, provoked resistance on the part of all opponents of the regime. Artisans and workers took to the barricades and in the 'Three Glorious Days' of 27–29 July compelled Charles X to flee his kingdom. Some of the insurgents were republicans. Still more were Bonapartists, and amidst the fighting, sections of the popular classes voiced their support for 'Napoleon II'. In the event, however, it was the liberal opposition headed by such as Thiers, Guizot and Rémusat, who imposed their solution as to who should take the place of the departed king. The Duke of Orleans was invited to become Louis Philippe, King of the French, and the July Monarchy was born. Its supporters in both Paris and the provinces reaped the spoils of office at the expense of the discredited Bourbon officials. All this time Louis Napoleon remained in Switzerland, performing his military exercises at Thun.

The July Monarchy never put down popular roots. It is misleading to think of the regime as a bourgeois monarchy, or of its head as a 'Citizen King'. Louis Philippe was indeed the son of the regicide Philippe Egalité, had fought in the revolutionary armies and travelled extensively in the United States, but he was no bourgeois. Nor was he the idiot that his critics made him out to be. (The great satirist Daumier represented him as the pear, *la poire*, which in French alluded simultaneously to his unfortunate shape and possible mental incapacity.) Intelligent, knowledgeable about finance and industry as well as foreign policy, Louis Philippe intended to rule as well as reign, as the constitution permitted. His government frustrated a plot on the part of the Duchess of Berry and other Legitimists (partisans of the older Bourbon line) to foment counter-revolution in the conservative west of France in 1832. But, however hostile to ultra-royalism, the July Monarchy had no aversion to aristocracy. It established a new oligarchy, representing wealthy landowners (many of whom were titled), rich bankers (often Protestants), prosperous businessmen and professionals. The July Monarchy, in short, was a regime of the notables. By reducing the property qualification to 200 francs a year and by lowering the voting age to twenty-five, the new electoral law may have doubled the franchise to around 166,000 electors, but it still excluded the great majority of the petty bourgeoisie as well as peasants and workers.

The conservative bias of the new regime did not go unchallenged. Even some of its initial backers, drawn more to the 'party of movement' than to the 'party of order', began to side with the republican opposition (the men of the *National* newspaper being a case in point). Republicans, themselves divided between moderates and radicals, agitated for further reform. From the earliest days, discontented peasants and artisans voiced their grievances, usually economic rather than political. Protest took many forms – against the forest laws, against high food prices, against taxes on wine. Distressed artisans in the Lyon silk industry staged a brief insurrection in November 1831. Strikes were rife, peaking in 1833–34.

From the point of view of the government, the most alarming development was the connection established between the republican societies and the nascent working-class movement. The *Société des droits de l'homme*, having successfully recruited among the artisans of Paris, brought them out onto the streets on the occasion of the funeral of one of Napoleon's generals, Lamarque, on 15 June 1832, an event commemorated by Victor Hugo in *Les Misérables*. The most serious uprising took place in Lyon in April 1834 where, after six days of fighting, some 300 people were killed. A sympathetic rising in Paris on 13 April, likewise provoked by the *Société des droits de l'homme*, was put down by troops under the command of the brutal Marshal Bugeaud. One of Daumier's most powerful lithographs records how a number of innocent occupants of a house in the rue Transnonain were killed in the process. Masterminding the whole repressive operation was the young Minister of the Interior, Adolphe Thiers, who in 1871 would have an even greater opportunity to display his talents for the crushing of popular revolution.

By 1835 the July Monarchy seemed to have weathered the worst storms. Another assassination attempt on the King provided the pretext for severe censorship of the press and tougher sentences in the courts. A regime which had faced sterner challenges had little difficulty in dealing with Louis Napoleon's abortive coup at Strasbourg in 1836. Nevertheless, it remained unpopular. As an ideology, Orleanism claimed to represent the *juste milieu*, a middle way between reaction and anarchic revolution. In reality it was an apology for the crude class interests of the well-to-do. Guizot, the regime's leading statesman, was the principal spokesman for French 'Victorian values'. In his view the middle classes were the repository of all virtue. The poor had only themselves to blame for their plight. The state might intervene in the economy to protect the interests of manufacturers (pure *laissez-faire* was strictly for the British) but it must never intervene in relations between factory owner and worker. To all who were excluded from the high 200-franc tax-paying qualification to vote, Guizot preferred the advice: 'Get rich'. Politics were the preserve of male property-owners. In 1840 the Chamber of Deputies numbered some of the richest men in France. The July Monarchy was elected on an extremely narrow political base. After the 1832 Reform Act in England, one out of twenty-five inhabitants had the right to vote. In France the proportion was one in 170. The vast majority of constituencies had fewer than 1,000 voters, most of whom were open to governmental bribery or bullying. According to Alexis de Tocqueville, under Guizot the French government acted 'like a private business, each member thinking of public affairs only in so far as they could be turned to his private profit.'[3] In the end, the regime was to pay dearly for its steadfast refusal to broaden its base to include at least some of the lower middle classes who had no objection in principle to a liberal order based on property.

After 1840, the year of Louis Napoleon's ill-fated Boulogne expedition, the political stability of the regime hardened into immobility. In the 1830s the semblance of political conflict was maintained by the parliamentary manoeuvres of ambitious politicians and ministerial reshuffles. The appointment of the Guizot–Soult cabinet in 1840 committed the July Monarchy to the pursuit of prosperity at home and a pacific foreign policy. The government won the elections of 1846, which allowed the high-minded Guizot (an austere Calvinist) to attribute his success to the correctness of his policies rather than to his judicious use of bribery. Its fate, however, was already being sealed by events taking place outside the rarefied circles of Orleanist high politics. A regime dedicated to the notion of prosperity found itself struggling with economic problems after the bad corn and potato harvests of 1846, brought about by atrocious weather. In 1847 food prices soared and rural protest rose apace. Industry was hit, too, and in manufacturing areas workers were faced with wage cuts and unemployment. A financial crisis, resulting from the collapse of the railway boom, compounded the misery. Discontent was widespread and an atmosphere of crisis pervasive.

Critics were not wanting to exploit the difficulties encountered by the regime. Legitimists had never accepted the usurper, Louis Philippe, even if few now favoured attempts to revive the *ancien régime* and fewer still – only the hardcore Ultras of the 'white' south and reactionary west – believed in recourse to armed struggle. Instead, Legitimism, championed by professional men like the lawyer Berryer (Louis Napoleon's defence counsel in 1840) as well as by the old landed aristocracy, increasingly based its appeal on religion. Catholicism, enjoying a remarkable revival by comparison with the dark days of the Terror, had a political potential which Legitimists were ready to utilise against the July Monarchy. 'Social' Catholics, defending the notion of an organic community and a paternalistic social order, could point to the misery tolerated, if not spawned, by the Orleanist 'get rich' mentality. In the battle to eliminate state control over Catholic schools, a major political issue of the 1840s, Legitimists were able to enlist the support of 'liberal' Catholics such as Montalembert, thus creating splits within the Orleanist oligarchy. Moreover, the power of Catholicism to unite across class lines was not confined to bringing together the Catholic bourgeoisie and the old aristocracy. In the rural west it could deliver mass peasant support, while in some urban areas, at least in the south, it could rally Catholic workers against their Protestant employers. It is true that, as men of property, most Legitimists were reluctant to consort too closely with the forces of popular revolution. On the contrary, they sided *de facto* with the July Monarchy in its concern to uphold 'order'. Nevertheless, they had little love for Louis Philippe, and in his moment of crisis in 1848 they were prepared to see him go.

The republican challenge was more serious. During the Restoration, republicanism had been more of a historical memory than a political force, its lore passed on by oral tradition and Carbonarist conspirators of the 1820s. In 1830 republicans had not been strong enough to prevail over the liberals, who continued to favour genuine constitutional monarchy. Disillusionment with the modest changes effected by the new regime stimulated a surge of republican political activity. clubs like *Aide toi, le ciel t'aidera* and the *Société des droits de l'homme* became the centres of republican activism. Newspapers such as *Le National* and *La Tribune* diffused republican propaganda. Moderates campaigned for the introduction of universal (meaning manhood) suffrage, while more radical republicans, admirers of Robespierre, Marat and Desmoulins, wanted to add social as well as political change to the agenda of reform. A still more extreme wing of republicanism, associated with the eternal conspirator Blanqui, identified with the insurrectionary aspect of the revolutionary tradition and did not shrink from advocating its cause by terrorist methods. The success with which republicans diffused their ideas among sections of the working populations of Paris and Lyon in the early 1830s has already been noted, as has the government's ability to contain the republican challenge. In 1839 another attempted coup by Blanqui and his supporters was foiled with as little difficulty as those of Louis Napoleon in 1836 and 1840.

In the 1840s republicans learned to moderate their language, though they remained split between the men of *Le National*, who were willing to cooperate with the official parliamentary opposition, the *gauche dynastique*, and the more radical wing headed by Ledru-Rollin and associated with the newspaper *La Réforme*. Republicans were never in a position to bring down the regime, having little support in the countryside and only limited appeal in the towns, but they articulated the disenchantment with the July Monarchy which by 1848 had become general, particularly in the ranks of the lower middle classes and among politically conscious artisans.

Many of the latter subscribed to socialist as well as republican doctrines. Karl Marx exaggerated when he said that the spectre of socialism was haunting Europe in 1848, as to a lesser extent did Tocqueville, when he claimed that a growing army of workers, led astray by pernicious socialist ideas, was determined to expropriate the rich. But collectivist notions were widely diffused in working-class circles. Utopian socialist thinkers, many of them in search of a revitalised Christianity, offered a wide range of panaceas for the problems of industrial society. Etienne Cabet, who regarded Christ as the real founder of his Icarian communist movement, was probably the most influential in working-class circles. Philippe Buchez preached a Christian socialism which reached an audience of workers via the newspaper *L'Atelier*, while the messianic writings of the ex-priest Lamennais were also read by the popular classes in town and country. Louis Blanc was another who drew inspiration from an egalitarian reading of the gospels. Well-known as the author of *L'Organisation du travail* (1839) and as a contributor to *La Réforme*, he spread the idea that the state should create public works and provide cheap credit to workers' cooperatives. Certainly, cooperation and mutualism made sense to skilled artisans – tailors, cobblers, cabinet-makers – who faced ruin with the spread of new production and marketing techniques.

For the Orleanist bourgeoisie, socialist and working-class protest was a frightening sign that the reds were about to take over. Many nervous contemporaries also equated the *classes laborieuses with the classes dangereuses*, the uprooted masses who had swarmed into the larger cities, especially Paris, where the population had swollen to over a million by 1848. Balzac spoke for many other bourgeois contemporaries when he described the urban masses as 'savages'.[4] In reality, modern historians have shown that there was virtually no connection between crime and collective action on the part of workers. The participants in the popular revolutions were not the criminals and vagrants but, most frequently, skilled workers and craftsmen from traditional artisan trades.[5] The point remains, however, that workers were far from content with their lot and that the Orleanist establishment was right to fear a challenge to its monopoly of power.

In the late 1840s the call for reform came from all sides, not just the Left. The narrowness of the electoral base of the July Monarchy was an affront to all the excluded sections of the middle classes, especially those patriotic and politically conscious elements who constituted the membership of the National Guard. Their patriotism was also tried by the regime's foreign policy which, having appeared first to be unduly subservient to British interests in the pursuit of an Anglo-French *entente* and then to favour Metternichian conservatism, no longer concerned itself with notions of grandeur. Disgust with a regime already tainted by corruption deepened when a series of political and sexual scandals broke amidst all the other troubles. The so-called 'bourgeois monarchy' found itself alienated from most of the bourgeoisie.

Yet, as with the Bourbons in 1830, its demise in 1848 was not a historical inevitability. It might have survived the social and economic crises and the mounting demand for change but for its own ineptitude in handling the reform movement. Prevented by law from holding public meetings, advocates of change initiated a series of 'banquets' at which 'toasts' could be substituted for speeches and where many 'onlookers' could be in attendance. The banquet campaign was never meant to be a prelude to the barricades, but the Guizot government refused to make any concessions. The final banquet, scheduled for 22 February and due to be held in the twelfth arrondissement, heartland of the *classes populaires*, was banned. The moderate republicans and leaders of the dynastic opposition who had organised the banquet campaign were prepared to comply with the order, but not so groups of workers and students, who flocked onto the streets. The next day, the National Guard demonstrated its solidarity with the cause of reform by refusing to disperse the crowd. Louis Philippe finally recognised that he had no choice but to part with Guizot. The jubilation of the crowd, however, gave way to anger when troops clashed with celebrating demonstrators in an incident which left twenty dead and fifty wounded. Barricades went up over the night of 23–24 February. The King's appointment of Marshal Bugeaud to take charge of the military situation served only to inflame passions further, since for Parisians of the popular classes his name evoked memories of the massacre of the rue Transnonain of 1834. Neither Molé nor Thiers nor even Barrot, leader of the *gauche dynastique*, could form a ministry acceptable to the crowd. Renewed street-fighting, which included an attack on the Tuileries Palace itself, left Louis Philippe shattered and convinced that he had no choice but to abdicate in favour of his grandson, the count of Paris, a mere boy of ten. The parliamentarians were willing to contemplate a regency but the Parisian insurgents were not. Nothing less than a republic would satisfy them. The year 1848 would not be allowed to go the same way as 1830, when revolution from the streets had toppled a monarch but failed to impose a republican regime. In the evening of 24 February a provisional government of the Republic was drawn up at the Hôtel de Ville under the effective leadership of the poet-politician Lamartine.

In his English exile, Louis Napoleon had no hand in the events which consigned the Bourbons to the rubbish heap of French history. But developments over the course of the year 1848 at last presented him with the opportunity to attain the power which he had sought hitherto with such conspicuous lack of success.

. . .

## LOUIS NAPOLEON'S RISE TO POWER

In fact the sudden collapse of the Orleanist monarchy came as more of a surprise to Louis Napoleon than it should have done, given his long-standing convictions about the inevitability of the demise of the regime, and, more recently, the receipt of reports from Persigny predicting the February crisis. His immediate reaction was one of indecision. Only after several days of hesitation did he resolve to make for Paris. He arrived on 28 February and offered his services to the provisional government. Lamartine and his colleagues were less than delighted: in a situation still fraught with danger they had no need of a Bonapartist rival in their midst. Louis Napoleon was therefore asked to leave France. Persigny wanted him to stay and fight but, after Ham, the pretender entertained few illusions about the virtues of martyrdom. He preferred to wait on events and by 2 March he was back in England. There he enrolled as a special constable at Marlborough Street police station to assist with the work of quelling the riots anticipated as a consequence of Chartist demonstrations scheduled for 10 April. On the day, his only arrest was a drunk woman. His English friends were baffled by his behaviour in this episode, but for French observers he had signalled that he was committed to 'order' rather than to further revolution.

Fear of disorder was widespread in France among the possessing classes after the February Revolution of 1848. The prince de Broglie was not alone in recalling that 'the Republic' conjured up memories of 'bloodshed, confiscation, terror and war'.[6] According to Tocqueville, Odilon Barrot went around looking like a man about to be hanged.[7] Thiers, appalled by the mounting revolutionary tide, suffered a nervous breakdown.[8] On the other hand, for many people – workers, democrats, socialists, feminists – 1848 promised to be a year of liberation, a 'springtime of peoples', the realisation of the brotherhood of man. Even the clergy seemed to welcome the Revolution and sprinkled holy water on the trees of liberty. In his purple and golden words, Lamartine captured the quintessentially romantic spirit of 1848 with what Marx called 'its illusions, its poetry, its visionary content, and its phrases'.[9]

It was soon apparent that the pessimists' appraisal of the situation was the more accurate. The new regime did not entirely lack talent or expertise. Lamartine was not a poet by profession but a diplomat and deputy, and six of his ministerial colleagues had also been deputies in the parliament of the July Monarchy. Some of the government's early measures were progressive. Manhood (often wrongly styled universal) suffrage was introduced. A decree of 25 February proclaimed the right to work. Freedom of the press and freedom of association were reintroduced. Slavery in the colonies was abolished, as was the death penalty for political offences. In a famous speech of 4 March, Lamartine, seeking to allay the fears of other powers, promised that the revolution was not for export. But the provisional government remained a fragile and ideologically divided entity. The majority (associated with the newspaper *Le National*) still clung to the tenets of economic liberalism. The more radical element, represented by the socialist Louis Blanc, the worker Albert and others, like Flocon, who had connections with *La Réforme*, was in a distinct minority. Lamartine occupied a centrist position, supported for the time being by the future radical leader Ledru-Rollin. Tensions were inherent from the start, and it had taken all of Lamartine's eloquence to prevent the red flag of the socialists from becoming the emblem of the Republic in the place of the tricolour.

What lent importance to this clash over symbols was the continuing urgency of the social and economic crisis. The most pressing problem was unemployment, and it was to tackle this that the government established a system of national workshops, which, however, fell far short of the model outlined by Louis Blanc in his *L'Organisation du travail*. To pay for the increased expenditure on the part of the state, direct taxation was increased by 45 per cent – a measure which provoked riots in the countryside, since it fell most heavily on peasants. In an overwhelmingly rural country, the land tax soon proved to be a costly political error.

Another problem for the new regime was the political ferment to which its very reforms gave rise (in the towns at least, and in Paris above all). A host of political clubs appeared and, with the inveterate conspirator Blanqui released from gaol, agitation returned to the streets. Demonstrations were staged on 17 March and 16 April. The government itself contributed to the process of politicisation since, contrary to what is sometimes alleged, it was well aware of the need to win over the great mass of new peasant voters. Elections to nominate a Constituent Assembly had been set for 23 April and Ledru-Rollin as Minister of the Interior organised a propaganda campaign throughout the provinces. If his efforts bore little fruit, it was in no small part because of resentment against the 45 per cent tax increase.

The election results were a disaster for the republican movement. Only about a third of the 900 seats went to republicans of the pre-February 1848 vintage. Most of the deputies turned out to be monarchists, even if they had prudently pledged support for the Republic during the election campaign. Election day had coincided with Easter Sunday, and many of the new voters had been conducted to the polls by their *curé* or local *seigneur*. The Constituent Assembly resurrected the notables as a political force. The new governmental team, or Executive Commission, retained largely the personnel of the provisional government but significantly did not include Louis Blanc or Albert. The left gave vent to its frustration in protest movements in a number of urban centres: Limoges, Rouen, but especially Paris. On 15 May an angry crowd invaded the Assembly to demonstrate its solidarity with the Polish uprising against the Tsar, while Blanqui also called for action to alleviate the sufferings of starving workers. Whether the incident was a genuine attempt at a coup or the work of *provocateurs* in the pay of the government remains a moot point. The upshot, however, was the arrest of the leaders of the left such as Blanqui, Barbès, Albert and Louis Blanc. Political opinion was now dangerously polarised between a frightened conservative majority, no longer interested in ideals of reconciliation and fraternity, but bent, rather, on the destruction of their enemies, and a minority of radicals, bitterly resentful of the way they seemed to have been cheated, once again, of the fruits of victory on the barricades. Further confrontation was inevitable.

Louis Napoleon well appreciated the deterioration in the situation. Among those who had been elected on 23 April were three members of his family (his cousins Napoleon-Jerome,

Pierre Bonaparte and Lucien Murat). It was clear that what had counted was the family name, for other Bonapartist candidates (including Persigny) were defeated. Despite some lingering doubts, Louis Napoleon allowed his own name to be put forward as a candidate in by-elections scheduled for 4 June. Under the system of *scrutin de liste*, whereby in each department electors chose from a slate of candidates, he was elected for Paris and the departments of the Seine, the Yonne, the Charente-Inférieure and Corsica. These electoral triumphs were followed by Bonapartist demonstrations in the streets of Paris, not all of which were spontaneous, since Bonapartist agents had infiltrated the national workshops and recruited among the unemployed. Lamartine's government was alarmed, and proposed banning him from taking his seat. The deputies refused their consent, but, in any case, for the time being, Louis Napoleon was content to remain in London, and on 16 June wrote to offer his resignation. Never, he declared, would he allow his name to be the pretext for disorder. Only after calm was restored would he return to France. His letter was well timed. A week later the pent-up fury of the workers was released in the social explosion of the June Days.

The workers' rising was touched off by the decision to close the national workshops on 22 June. It was a spontaneous revolt, fuelled by a deep-seated sense of betrayal and recognisable to both Marx and Tocqueville as naked class war. Barricades were erected in eastern Paris on 23 June and three days of savage street fighting began. Artisans, labourers and a certain number of small employers were pitted against regular troops commanded by the Minister of Defence, General Cavaignac, supported by bourgeois National Guardsmen and 12,000 *gardes mobiles*, a body of younger, unskilled and unemployed workers. One thousand five hundred insurgents were killed, 12,000 arrested. With the defeat of the workers' movement died the ideals of February. Full-scale reaction was implemented by the government, now headed by General Cavaignac, the victor of the June Days. Controls were established over the political clubs and the press. Veteran Orleanist, and even Legitimist, politicians easily regained their ascendancy at the expense of the inexperienced deputies of the Assembly. And, to consolidate the restoration of order by ensuring strong central government, on 4 November 1848 the Assembly opted for a constitution in which executive power was concentrated in the hands of a president elected by manhood suffrage while the single-chamber legislature exercised only legislative functions. A system better suited to the ambitions of Louis Napoleon it would have been hard to devise.

By September, when a second round of by-elections was due, Louis Napoleon had decided that the time was ripe for his return to France. He entered himself as a candidate in thirteen departments and was returned by five. In Paris, where he topped the poll, he obtained 110,000 votes. His campaign managers were told to give no hint of any aspirations to bring back the Empire, and to stress his patriotism, his desire to serve the Republic and, perhaps most significantly, his commitment to order. He arrived in Paris on 24 September to take his seat for the department of the Yonne. His maiden speech, delivered in a thin voice and German-sounding accent, did not impress an Assembly accustomed to the cadences of polished orators, but it did not altogether allay the suspicions of deputies who doubted his protests of loyalty to the Republic. In the constitutional debates, his future hung in the balance, for there were those who wished to have the President of the Republic elected by the Assembly itself – an eventuality which would have doomed Louis Napoleon's candidacy to failure. It was not he but Lamartine who, in a stirring speech, swung opinion in the Assembly behind the idea of a presidency elected by manhood suffrage, and thus kept Bonapartist hopes alive.

Even so, he faced another danger when on 9 October a motion was put forward to ban members of former ruling dynasties from standing as presidential candidates. Stung into replying personally, he stammered out his objections so ineffectually that the author of the amendment withdrew his proposal on the grounds that it was clearly superfluous. Indifferent to the contempt of more eloquent deputies, Louis Napoleon knew that silence would serve his immediate purpose more readily than eloquence. He therefore maintained an aloof reserve from the Chamber until he was ready to announce his candidature for the Presidency of the Republic on 26 October.

The result of the election, held on 10 December 1848, was a sensation, even if it was never seriously in doubt. Louis Napoleon's principal rival was Cavaignac, the hope of the moderate republicans, but a man who, despite his severity in repressing the June insurrection, was deemed to be too liberal by the truly conservative elements. He polled fewer than 1.5

million votes. The conservatives, now ready to shelve their ideological differences in defence of property (a trend encapsulated in the conversion of the former anticlerical Thiers to the virtues of Catholic education) could not field a candidate of their own without reopening dynastic disagreements between Orleanists and Legitimists and reluctantly looked to Louis Napoleon as the likeliest guarantor of order. Besides, they assumed that he was a dolt who could be led by the nose. Radical republicans preferred Ledru-Rollin to Cavaignac, massacrer of the workers, though more intransigent and socialist-inclined members of the left favoured Raspail. Ledru-Rollin obtained 371,000 votes, Raspail 37,000. Lamartine, too, entered the lists, as did General Changarnier on behalf of die-hard Legitimists. The former could muster only 18,000 votes, the latter not even 500.[10]

None of these candidates stood a chance against the only man whose name meant something to the rural masses who constituted three-quarters of the population, and who voted for him not simply out of deference to the inclinations of their social superiors but more from a conviction that he alone could be their saviour in a time of acute crisis. In many parts of the countryside, Louis Napoleon benefited from a popular Bonapartism which was now profoundly anti-republican, on account of the Republic's association with continuing misery and disorder. At the same time, it retained its egalitarian aspirations and hatred of 'the rich'. A Bonapartism of the left could be discerned in the Limousin, Périgord, the Dauphiné and several departments in the centre of France, such as the Cher and the Nièvre. In the Isère, it seems that there were peasants who believed that they were voting for the uncle rather than the nephew, but the crucial point was that they were expressing their faith in a Bonaparte as the best guarantee against any return to the *ancien régime*. The Pretender's propaganda reached ordinary people less through the written word – he had a majority of the newspapers against him – than by the means best-suited to penetrate popular culture: images, posters, medals, engravings, songs (often evoking the theme of the messianic return), all of which were skilfully diffused by itinerant agents at fairs and markets in the countryside.

Louis Napoleon won 5.5 million votes, 74.2 per cent of the poll. Even in the towns, not excluding Paris, voters were susceptible to Bonapartist populism. In the capital, where he polled

58 per cent of the vote, Louis Napoleon's electors were as numerous in the working-class suburbs of eastern Paris as in the elegant bourgeois *quartiers*.[11] The author of *Napoleonic Ideas* and *The Extinction of Poverty* (the latter reissued whole and in extracts as part of his electoral propaganda) had not been wrong to place his faith in the people. Manhood suffrage presented him with the power which he had sought in vain by conspiracy. Louis Napoleon's rise to power was one of the more ironic consequences of the advent of democratic politics in France between 1815 and 1848.

. . .

## NOTES AND REFERENCES

1. The authoritative study of this theme is now Ménager B 1988 *Les Napoléons du peuple*
2. For the distinction between the myth and the legend, see Bluche F 1980 *Le Bonapartisme 1800–1850*, p. 168ff
3. Tocqueville A de 1959 (ed Mayer J P) *Recollections*, Meridian, p. 5
4. Chevalier L 1973 (French edn, 1958) *Labouring and Dangerous Classes in Paris during the First Half of the Nineteenth Century*. Routledge & Kegan Paul
5. Critics of Chevalier include Rudé G 1973 'Cities and Popular Revolt', in Bosher J (ed) *French Government and Society 1500–1850*. London University Press
6. Quoted by Bury J P T 1985 (5th edn; 1st edn, 1949) *France 1814–1940*. Methuen, p. 71
7. Tocqueville *Recollections*, p. 46
8. Ibid., p. 58. On Thiers, see Bury J P T and Tombs R P 1986 *Thiers 1797–1877: a Political Life*. Allen & Unwin
9. Marx K 1937 (1st edn, 1850) *The Class Struggles in France 1848–1850*. Martin Lawrence, p. 39. See also *The Eighteenth Brumaire of Louis Bonaparte*. International Publishers, 1926 (1st edn, 1852)
10. Tudesq A J 1965 *L'Election présidentielle de Louis-Napoléon Bonaparte 10 décembre 1848*
11. Ménager 1988, pp. 102–5

# Chapter 4

# FROM THE ELYSEE TO THE TUILERIES (1848–52)

On 20 December 1848, Louis Napoleon was formally invested as the President of the Second French Republic. He was forty years old. For thirty-three years he had lived in exile or in prison: now the failed conspirator and ex-prisoner headed the executive power in France. To the deputies of the National Assembly he cut a bizzare, un-Napoleonic figure who spoke French with a German accent. Standing less than 5.5 feet tall, he had a body that was too long for his short legs and a head that sank into his shoulders. His complexion was pallid, his grey eyes dull and glassy. His most prominent features were his large nose, thin military moustache and pointed beard (which made him an easy target for caricaturists). A cosmopolitan in the midst of provincials, he exuded an air of *ennui* and lack of energy, while his well-known commitment to the pleasures of the flesh and social life accentuated the impression of indolence. Rising at 10 a.m., he would while away the morning before presiding over cabinet meetings between 1300 and 1500 hours, after which he was free to consort with Miss Howard, who had followed him to Paris. He was easy to underestimate, and most of the leading politicians did so. Thiers called him a 'cretin'. Montalembert was exceptional in recognising how ill-founded was his reputation for incapacity.[1]

* * *

## PRESIDENT OF THE REPUBLIC

Although elected by an overwhelming majority of the French male population, the Prince President was virtually unknown in his own country. In particular, he had no friends among the French *classe politique*. Republican politicians remained suspicious of his ultimate aims, despite his solemn oath 'to remain faithful to the democratic Republic and to defend the Constitution'. Neither Cavaignac nor Lamartine was prepared to serve as his premier. Given that few of his immediate entourage were fit for ministerial office, he turned to the 'party of order' to staff his cabinet. Thiers, hoping no doubt to succeed him after four years, declined office but was profuse with backstairs advice. On his recommendations Odilon Barrot was appointed prime minister and a number of his personal protégés were given ministerial posts. As an important sop to Catholic opinion, the Legitimist Falloux was appointed Minister of Public Instruction and Religion. Louis Napoleon was not entirely happy about having to settle for a government team made up of the 'second eleven', but for the time being he could do little about the situation. Emile Ollivier called this first cabinet *'le ministère de la captivité'*, and it is true that for his first year in office the Prince President, if not condemned to impotence, as Persigny claimed, was circumscribed in his exercise of power.[2] In the words of one biographer, he presided, but did not govern.[3]

From the start, however, Louis Napoleon demonstrated that he had no intentions of remaining a tool of his ministers. One of his first executive acts was to send for the files on his attempted coups at Strasbourg and Boulogne, which provoked the resignation of the Minister of the Interior Malleville. Nor was he ready to brook obstruction from the Assembly, which, partly from a reluctance to recognise that its role was over and partly from fear of a presidential *coup d'état*, refused to dissolve itself to allow fresh elections to be held. In confrontations between the Assembly and Barrot (who found its leanings still too republican for his taste) Louis Napoleon backed his ministers. Thus he refused to accept Barrot's resignation when it was tendered after he had failed to persuade the Assembly to adopt a measure to outlaw a number of radical clubs. When the clashes which punctuated the month of January 1849 threatened to produce agitation on the streets, on the night of 28 January 1849 Louis called out the National Guard and a body of regular troops. The impressive show of force compelled the Assembly to capitulate, though its fears of a Bonapartist coup were heightened. (They were not unjustified: some of the Prince's closest advisers were urging such a course of action upon him.) Not only was the Assembly brought to heel, but once again Louis Napoleon upheld his own authority over the cabinet. He needed the 'Party of Order', but it needed him more.

If the Prince President was intent on establishing his mastery over his ministers and the Assembly, he was even more determined to keep his own entourage under his control. Thus on the morrow of his electoral victory he rejected the advice of the impetuous Persigny who favoured an immediate *coup d'état*. Nor was he tempted to stage a premature *putsch* by the arguments of General Changarnier or his half-brother Morny on the strength of the Bonapartist sentiments evident among National Guardsmen on the night of 28/29 January. When his cousin Prince Napoleon also hinted that he ought to launch a coup, once again Louis Napoleon stood firm, expressing his refusal in terms which left no doubt about his determination to exercise personal power. In a letter dated 10 April 1849 he wrote:

> I shall never submit to any attempt to influence me, and shall always make it my business to govern in the interests of the people, not of any party. I respect those whose ability and experience enable them to give me good advice.... But I follow only the promptings of my mind and heart.... Nothing, nothing shall trouble the clear vision of my judgement or the strength of my resolution. I shall march straight forward with no moral scruples in the path of honour, with conscience my only guide.[4]

Given such an outlook, Louis Napoleon could hardly fail to make his own impact on government policy.

On the domestic front, the problem which most exercised the 'party of order' was the suppression of the 'reds', and Louis Napoleon did not fail to impress on them that he alone was qualified for the task. That political divisions in the country had deepened since the elections of April 1848 was evident in the campaign which preceded the elections of 13 May 1849, called after the Constituent Assembly finally agreed to dissolve itself. Opinion was polarised between the implacable conservatives of the 'party of order', embracing monarchists of all shades but including most Bonapartists, and 'red' republicans, committed to the democratic and social republic and led by Ledru-Rollin. In numerical terms, the election result was a crushing victory for the reactionaries, who gained nearly 500 of the 750 seats in the legislature. But the fact that the radical republicans returned around 200 deputies was more than enough to strike fear into the hearts of the victors. What terrified them most was not the predictable leftward leanings of the workers of Paris and Lyon, but the sizeable 'red' vote in a number of rural departments, which raised the prospect in the future of the countryside engulfed by 'socialism'. The vanquished *démoc-socs* were by no means downcast by the election results, while the victorious conservatives were panic-stricken. In these circumstances, Louis Napoleon was well placed to present himself as the 'saviour of society'.

Retaining Barrot as his premier, he wrote to him to insist that

> the first necessity is to impose on affairs a precise and energetic direction. We need men devoted to my very person, from the deputies to the police inspectors.... We have to keep everyone's actions under surveillance... We need finally to reawaken everywhere the memory not of the Empire but of the Emperor, for that is the only sentiment by means of which subversive ideas can be combated.[5]

Barrot had little time for Louis Napoleon's invocations of the Empire, but he was prepared to collaborate with him in the work of suppressing the *démoc-socs*.

First, however, Louis Napoleon had a good opportunity to consolidate his credibility with conservatives over an issue of foreign policy, namely that of how France should react to the revolutionary events which had been taking place in the Italian peninsula. By the spring of 1849 the challenge of the Italian patriots to Habsburg rule in the north had been repressed by the military might of Austria. Only the Roman Republic, established in February 1849 after the flight of Pope Pius IX to Gaeta, remained as a symbol of hope for Jacobins in Italy and abroad. But when the Pope appealed to the Catholic powers of Europe to restore him to his throne, the dilemma for French policy became acute. Successive foreign ministers of the Second Republic, acting in concert with Palmerston, had successfully sought to limit the damage inflicted on Piedmont by the victorious Austrians, but the question of the Roman Republic was more intractable. Louis Napoleon, hostile to the extension of Austrian influence in the peninsula and sympathetic to Italian nationalist aspirations in the Papal States, had no wish to see the Pope restored by force of Austrian arms. On the other hand, as a champion of order, he could not risk alienating his conservative supporters by encouraging Italian Jacobins. In particular, he could not alienate Catholic opinion in France at a time when prominent Catholic leaders such as Montalembert and the abbé Dupanloup were urging him to restore Pius IX to the throne of Peter. Louis Napoleon did the only thing possible in the circumstances. He equivocated.

His instincts were to turn to 'conference diplomacy' in the hope that the 'European concert' could find a solution.[6] His preference was for a general European conference, but, failing that, he was willing to submit the Roman Question to a conference which had already convened at Brussels to address the dispute between Austria and Piedmont-Sardinia. The main idea which emerged from Brussels was that France should join with Britain in trying to negotiate acceptable solutions to the problems of northern Italy. The suggestion appealed to Louis Napoleon, but not to the British. He therefore turned to another conference of 'Catholic' powers (France, Spain, Austria and the Two Sicilies) which met at Gaeta at the end of March as the best hope for a peaceful settlement, but the Austrians, flushed with their recent success at the battle of Novara on 23 March, were not willing to make real concessions. Neither was Pius IX. In the end, Louis had only three choices: to abandon the Pope, to let Austria act alone or to initiate action by France.[7] He chose the last.

A task force commanded by General Oudinot was sent on 25 April, though its precise mission still remained unclear. Probably the French government was hoping to save the Pope's temporal power while at the same time obliging him to accept constitutional reforms. What would happen should neither the Mazzinians nor Pius IX conform to the role assigned to them by French foreign policy was not properly considered. In the event, the leaders of the Roman Republic rejected French mediation and, inspired by Garibaldi, beat off Oudinot's assault on 30 April. French radicals, outraged that a sister republic should come under attack from French arms, loudly protested that they had been duped as to the real purpose of the expedition. Louis Napoleon, however, stung by the slight to French military honour, decided to reinforce the French presence, though, still treading a precarious path between Catholic and Jacobin opinion at home, he also dispatched an emissary in the person of Ferdinand de Lesseps, the future builder of the Suez Canal, to pursue diplomatic negotiations. De Lesseps struck an agreement with Mazzini whereby the Roman people were to decide their own fate after a referendum supervised by French troops. But after the elections of 13 May, such a solution was unacceptable to the reactionaries who dominated the Legislative Assembly. De Lesseps was recalled and charged with exceeding his instructions which in turn provoked the radicals to take to the streets in a peaceful demonstration on 13 June. The turnout was small, but in any case it was met by a show of force on the part of the government in which Louis Napoleon personally took part alongside Changarnier's National Guard. The French Mountain was routed, and Ledru-Rollin forced into hiding and exile. Protests outside of Paris, notably in Lyon, were brutally repressed. In a proclamation to the French people, Louis Napoleon spelled out his hard-line attitude. 'It is time,' he declared, 'that good men should be reassured, and that bad men should tremble.'[8] Oudinot renewed his attack on Rome and on 3 July French troops entered the Eternal City. French Catholics were delighted. Louis Napoleon was less ecstatic, especially when he realised that the Pope intended to have no truck with liberalism or constitutional government. To register his discontent he wrote a letter on 18 August to his friend Colonel Edgar Ney to complain about the way in which a French army had become an instrument of despotism rather than an agent of liberation. The letter was immediately leaked, and provoked not only displeasure at the Curia but Falloux's resignation from the government. In counting on a *rapprochement* between the Papacy and liberty, Louis Napoleon had badly miscalculated and for the rest of his political life he would find no escape from the complications of 'the Roman Question'.

Nevertheless, in the short term he was able to turn the Roman expedition and its consequences to his political advantage. On 31 October he decided to rid himself of the Barrot ministry on the grounds that his ministers were obstructive and out of sympathy with his aims, as was evident in their failure to respond to the sentiments he had expressed in his letter to Ney. A firm hand had to be set on the tiller of government. Hitherto there had been too much discord among conflicting parties. Now he wanted men 'who are as preoccupied with my own responsibility as with theirs'. The country wanted firm direction from the man who had been elected on 10 December. His very

name was in itself a whole programme, implying order, authority, religion and the well-being of the people at home, and
'national dignity' abroad.[9] Louis Napoleon had finally established his dominance over the executive power and was in a
position to rule as well as reign. To confirm his ascendancy, he
brought into the government team new men such as the lawyer
Rouher (Minister of Justice) and the banker Achille Fould
(Minister of Finance). Ferdinand Barrot accepted the Ministry
of the Interior and was immediately dubbed Cain for his
treachery towards his better-known brother Odilon. There was
no real prime minister. The Prince President directed affairs.

The royalists who formed a majority of the Legislative
Assembly were unhappy with the change of governmental
personnel and with the new presidential style of rule. In their
eyes Louis Napoleon was an adventurer and an upstart whose
right even to call himself a Bonaparte was questionable, given
the well-known marital infidelities of Hortense. His presence at
the Elysée had been tolerated only as a temporary expedient
prior to a monarchist restoration. But Louis Napoleon had
shown that he was determined to be no one's creature. The
potential for conflict was real, especially if the 'red menace'
which had promoted the marriage of convenience in the first
place should recede. For the time being, however, the uneasy
alliance continued, and one of its fruits was the passing of the
Falloux Law.

One of the issues which had divided the *notables* under the
July Monarchy was the question of 'freedom of education'; that
is, the question of Catholic schools in relation to the University,
the body established by Napoleon in 1808 to be responsible for
all levels of the educational system. In the 1840s, led by
Montalembert, Catholic spokesmen mounted a determined
assault on the University's monopoly, denying the right of the
state to interfere with the educational institutions of the Church.
Successive Ministers of Public Instruction refused to bow to this
pressure and denounced 'clerical' attempts to subvert the
authority of the state. The quarrel had not been resolved when
the July Monarchy was overthrown in February 1848. The
events of that year, above all the June Days, produced a
dramatic change of heart among the defenders of the University.
Almost overnight, Voltairean sceptics such as Thiers conceded
the wisdom of assigning a special role to the Church in the fight
against anarchy and red revolution. Teachers in state primary

schools were denounced as republican agitators who were poisoning the minds of the nation's youth. Just as Louis Napoleon needed the 'party of order', so the 'party of order' discovered that it needed the Church. The price of its support, extracted by Falloux as Minister of Public Instruction, was concessions with regard to both primary and secondary education. Following the report of a commission chaired by Thiers and including prominent representatives of the Catholic and University worlds, a law was passed on 15 March 1850 which favoured the expansion of schools run by religious orders at the primary level and which recognised the principle of 'freedom of education' at the secondary level.

The enactment of the Falloux Law was a spectacular example of the conservative response to the threat of social revolution, but it was only one of a series of measures taken by the President and the reactionary majority in parliament against the *démoc-socs*. New republican successes at the polls intensified the fears of the reactionaries. On 10 March 1850, in the by-elections held to replace the *montagnard* deputies disbarred for their participation in the affair of 13 June, eleven out of twenty-one seats were retained by the reds, including all three of the Paris seats. Another victory for the left in a subsequent by-election in Paris held on 28 April (where the popular novelist Eugène Sue defeated the National Guardsman Leclerc, who had fought against the insurgents of the June Days) confirmed the worst misgivings of the conservatives about the pernicious effects of manhood suffrage. The left had to be crushed, and a law of 31 May was passed to deprive it of electoral support. By introducing technical grounds on which large numbers of (mainly poor) people could be disqualified from voting, some 2.5 million voters were removed from the rolls in an attempt to ensure an electoral triumph for the right in the legislative elections due to be held in 1852. The repressive powers of a centralised bureaucratic state were also brought to bear against radicals and democrats. Hundreds of mayors were dismissed and municipal councils dissolved. In larger urban areas martial law was imposed when other methods of political repression – the arrest of militants, surveillance and disruption of meetings, restriction of press freedom – were deemed to be inadequate. *Démoc-soc* organisation was smashed and activists driven to an underground existence, though in a number of rural departments in the centre and south it is possible that the repression was ineffective for lack of police manpower and because it stiffened local resistance to interference on the part of the state.

The taming of the 'reds' was a matter of satisfaction to the reactionaries, but it had the additional consequence of bringing into the open the differences which existed between them and Louis Napoleon. 'Cohabitation' was no longer necessary, and he could safely be ditched, particularly since the constitution denied him the right to run for re-election in 1852. The prospect of seeing his political career terminated before it had hardly begun did not appeal to the Prince President. Increasingly, his thoughts turned to dispensing with his treacherous allies of the *parti de l'ordre* and to effecting constitutional change which would allow him to remain in office. For some time Louis Napoleon had been assiduously building up both his personal authority and his popularity. He made important changes of personnel in the administrative services, involving prefects, ambassadors and army officers. To cultivate different sections of public opinion he granted amnesties to deportees of June 1848, increased the pay of junior officers and entertained lavishly at the Elysée (senior military men were made specially welcome). He also went on extensive provincial tours, which, as in July 1850, included areas of the east of France loyal to republicanism. In September, in the more congenial atmosphere of conservative Normandy, he was more explicit about his ultimate personal ambitions, expressing his willingness to assume a monarchical role should that be deemed in the best interests of the country.

Yet he was still not committed to a *coup d'état*. The objective was constitutional revision to permit him to stand again for the presidency of the Republic. To this end, through his prefects, he tried to persuade the general councils of the departments to mount a campaign for constitutional change. Two-thirds responded favourably, but it was not the overwhelming majority he needed. At the same time the Assembly was becoming more truculent. Louis Napoleon's largesse and his propaganda efforts had landed him with serious debts and he and his Finance Minister Fould wished the Assembly to increase his 'entertainment allowance' by 2.4 million francs, a suggestion which the deputies indignantly threw out before agreeing to a compromise. The honeymoon between Louis Napoleon and the Assembly was almost over and the time for a trial of strength close.

As both Louis Napoleon and his conservative allies realised, the key to power was the army, and in particular the figure of General Changarnier, who as commander of the First Military Division and commander-in-chief of the National Guard in the department of the Seine had control of all troops in the Paris area. A royalist increasingly disenchanted with Louis Napoleon (to whom he referred as 'the melancholy parrot'), he had close links with leading conservatives in the Assembly and was keen to suppress Bonapartist sentiments in the army. At the beginning of January 1851 Louis Napoleon sacked him, and all the protests of the deputies were powerless to save him. When his ministers tendered their resignations the Prince President appointed a new team made up of men little known but entirely devoted to himself. To appease the Assembly, Louis Napoleon described the new ministry as transitional and carried out a re-shuffle on 10 April to bring in Léon Faucher as Minister of the Interior. (As one of the authors of the disenfranchisement law of 31 May, he was a reassuring figure for the conservatives, though he was prepared to help the President obtain the revision of the constitution which he desired.) But if Faucher was the best-known figure in the government, Louis Napoleon's friends – Baroche, Rouher, Magne – were also in place. Even more significantly, he began to cultivate the notorious General Saint-Arnaud, a reckless adventurer, libertine and scourge of 'reds', who burst into public prominence in June 1851 following his brutal repression of revolt in Algeria. Louis Napoleon rewarded him by promoting him to Major-General and trans-ferring him to a senior military post close to Paris. In November 1851 he was made Minister of War. Louis Napoleon was ultimately able to replace Changarnier with a more reliable general.

After the Changarnier affair, rumours were rife of an impend-ing coup. Yet Louis Napoleon was reluctant to take such drastic action. In the spring and summer of 1851 he had not aban-doned the hope that constitutional revision could be achieved by legal means. He was encouraged by the disarray now mani-fest in the ranks of the conservatives, divided not only over how far to support Changarnier (a majority found themselves voting with the left against Louis Napoleon's new ministry) but also over the dynastic question itself, which had resurfaced after the death of Louis Philippe in August 1850. In July 1851, however, his hopes were dashed when, mobilised by Thiers, the monarchist groups in the Assembly mustered sufficient coherence to deny him the 75 per cent majority required to make a constitutional change, though a motion which would have allowed the President of the Republic to stand for a second term of office was carried by 446 votes to 278 on 19 July. A showdown there had to be, and from July 1851 the veteran conspirator was again plotting a *coup d'état*.

The crucial question now was only the matter of timing. Louis Napoleon consulted his closest advisers – his private secretary Mocquard, Persigny, Morny, Rouher, Prefect of Police Carlier and General Magnan, Changarnier's replacement as military commander in Paris – and a plan was drawn up to strike in September, during the parliamentary recess. This, however, was opposed by Saint-Arnaud who, though favourably disposed to a coup, did not like the idea of moving while the deputies were free to organise resistance in their localities. As the Assembly was not due to reconvene until 4 November, Louis Napoleon considered how best to distance himself further from his erstwhile conservative allies and on 8 October suddenly announced his commitment to the restoration of manhood suffrage and the repeal of the law of 31 May 1850. From the ministerial crisis which followed he took the opportunity to place his own men in key posts – mainly a team of civil servants but including Saint-Arnaud at the War Office. He also acquired a new Prefect of Police in place of Carlier, namely Maupas, formerly an unscrupulous Sub-prefect at Toulouse who faced possible criminal charges as a result of his misconduct in trying to frame radical elements in his department. Louis Napoleon was now perfectly positioned to stage his coup, for not only had he provoked the 'party of order' but he had also thrown the republicans into confusion by his Machiavellian manoeuvre to restore universal male suffrage. Moreover, he believed from his extensive tours of the provinces that the Assembly had little support in the country at large and could easily be represented as an obstacle to his reform plans, while the insecurities engendered by the combined impact of the lingering economic crisis, the ravages of a cholera epidemic and the spectre of massive 'red' gains in the elections of 1852 (notwithstanding the severity of the repression of the left since June 1848) all seemed to designate a Bonaparte as the saviour of society.

Even so, Louis Napoleon hesitated. Meticulous plans had already been made by Morny, but Louis Napoleon wanted to wait first to see the outcome of the debate on his proposal to amend the electoral law. It lost narrowly on 15 November by 353 votes to 347, with the republicans having voted with Bonapartists in opposition to the conservatives. Two days later he was ready to move, pending the result of a debate initiated by the conservatives on whether the Assembly should appoint three deputies as 'quaestors' to mobilise the army on behalf of the Assembly should the House feel that its security was in jeopardy. That it had every reason to be alarmed was evident from a circular sent by Saint-Arnaud to all generals reminding them ominously of the need for strict military discipline and absolute obedience to orders. The republican deputies, however, more afraid of a royalist than a Bonapartist coup, voted with the supporters of the President to defeat the motion to appoint the quaestors. Their fears may not have been altogether spurious – royalist intrigues seem to have been afoot in northern France – but evidence of their miscalculation was not long in coming. Having postponed the date of the *putsch* yet again on 20 November and 25 November in the hope of reaching a last-minute deal with the 'party of order' on revision of the constitution, he settled finally for 2 December. It may be that, as Palmerston believed, his hand was forced in the end by the need to act before the royalists themselves struck.[10] But it is even more likely that he had opted to have his date with destiny on the anniversary of Austerlitz and of Napoleon I's coronation. All the evidence suggests that in 1851 Louis Napoleon was a reluctant *putschist*, but it is hard to see what alternative was open to him if he were to retain power and go on to fulfil his self-appointed mission. Operation 'Rubicon' – Louis Napoleon's own code name for the coup – merely awaited his signal. At midnight on 1–2 December he gave it.

During the night proclamations justifying the coup were prepared at the Imprimerie Nationale. At dawn some seventy-eight arrests were made, mainly of left republicans but including fourteen deputies. Saint-Arnaud's troops occupied the Chamber of Deputies and took up strategic positions in Paris. A personal order from Louis Napoleon to a battalion commander of the National Guard had led to the sabotaging of its drums and powder supplies, thus ensuring that no immediate call to resistance would come from that quarter. Morny took over at the Ministry of the Interior. By 7 a.m. on 2 December Persigny could inform his master that the coup had been a complete success. 'Rubicon' had not suffered the fate of Strasbourg and Boulogne.

What the conspirators had not reckoned on, however, was the widespread resistance which the *putsch* provoked. Louis Napoleon had gambled on his own popularity being recognised as infinitely superior to that of the Assembly. An 'Appeal to the People' stated that the Assembly, instead of being a force for order, was itself a hotbed of conspiracy, and had therefore been dissolved, leaving the public to judge between it and himself. But not only did the deputies still at liberty put up more opposition than anticipated on the morrow of the coup, which led to further arrests (Tocqueville, Rémusat, Barrot, Falloux and Berryer among them), but their actions helped to engender resistance among the ordinary working people of Paris, already being exhorted to take to the barricades by more leftist, *montagnard* deputies. On 3 December a clash between troops and workers in the faubourg Saint-Antoine left one soldier and two civilians dead, one of them the deputy Baudin. On 4 December barricades went up in earnest and once again the popular classes defended their liberties with their blood, this time with much more sympathy from the bourgeois *quartiers*, all the more so when the middle classes discovered that the troops were as ready to fire on bourgeois as on workers. On the *grands boulevards* some thirty-five innocent onlookers were cut down alongside 100 insurgents. By the end of the day, Morny was master of the situation, but for Victor Hugo and others this was the 'crime' for which Louis Napoleon could never know forgiveness.[11]

Most shocking of all to the Bonapartists was the scale of resistance in the provinces. In south-eastern France and in some departments of the centre and the south-west peasants, workers and republicans who had been at the sharp end of severe governmental repression since 1849 rose up in a massive wave of protest, mingling local grievances with indignation at the violation of the constitution on the part of a president sworn to uphold it. As many as 100,000 individuals were involved, though they were quickly overpowered by the military forces deployed to crush them. But such widespread opposition frightened the *parti de l'ordre* as much as it dismayed Louis Napoleon. The nightmare of a rural *jacquerie* and of sweeping *démoc-soc* gains in the legislative elections of 1852 allowed Louis Napoleon to reconstitute his alliance with the forces of the right. Paradoxically, a coup perpetrated allegedly to protect the people against the machinations of the Assembly quickly came to be justified as a preventive measure to quell rural disorder. The defeat of the insurrection was therefore followed by massive proscriptions. More than 26,000 *démoc-socs* were arrested. The least fortunate were the 239 transported to Devil's Island in French Guiana; 9,500 were deported to Algeria, some 3,000 imprisoned and another 5,000 placed under police surveillance. Martial law was imposed on thirty-two departments until the end of March 1852. Louis Napoleon himself had little relish for repression of such magnitude, and intervened personally to have several thousand sentences revised. In secret he tried to provide money for the families of victims. To the end of his days, thoughts of 2 December would return to haunt and depress him. He paid a high price for the manner by means of which he succeeded in perpetuating himself in power. For the longer term, he had opened a breach between himself and a substantial section of the political nation. The victims of the purge included articulate and literate bourgeois as well as peasants – people well able to express their deep antipathy to Louis Napoleon's new regime.

In the short run, however, he had succeeded in attaining his goal of maintaining himself in power. A plebiscite held on 20 December 1851 overwhelmingly endorsed his action by 7.5 million votes to 640,000, with 1.5 million abstentions. While it is true that martial law and repression prevented the full extent of the opposition from being revealed, it seems clear that the plebiscite confirmed the potency of the Napoleonic myth, now fused with the Bonapartist cause as personified by Louis Napoleon. By comparison with the presidential election of 1848, the Bonapartist vote had increased by 20 per cent. Support was strongest in the north-east of the country, where the economic situation seems to have been the decisive factor. Agricultural producers and workers in the large industrial centres alike seem to have been impatient for an end to the crisis. Popular Bonapartism also remained buoyant in most of its strongholds such as the Isère, where the workers of Grenoble were much more enthusiastic than the business community, though there was a certain falling off of support in other 'red' areas like the Limousin, where *démoc-soc* propaganda had begun to produce results. For many ordinary people, Napoleon stood for the consolidation of the revolutionary tradition and the defence of the national honour without the turmoil associated with the

Republic. The plebiscite revealed him to be, in large measure, a 'Napoleon of the people'.[12]

. . .

## THE RESTORATION OF THE EMPIRE

Few doubted that the *coup d'état* and the plebiscite were a prelude to the restoration of the Empire. As a herald of things to come the regime began to take on all the trappings of monarchy. Louis Napoleon was addressed as 'His Imperial Highness' and surrounded by a court. A new constitution, proposed in outline in the plebiscite of 20 December, was promulgated on 14 January 1852. Repudiating the original constitution of the Second Republic, which Louis Napoleon had sworn to uphold only three years previously, it confirmed 'Prince Louis Napoleon Bonaparte' in office for ten years and assigned him massive executive powers to command the armed forces, declare war, conclude peace treaties and alliances, and to make laws. He also appointed and dismissed ministers, who were obliged to take an oath of loyalty to him. The legislators, too, had to swear an oath of loyalty and were given only very limited powers. The upper chamber was nominated by the President, and sat in secret. The lower house, elected by manhood suffrage, was deprived of the right to question ministers, who could not themselves be deputies, and it was entitled only to reject, but not modify, executive legislation. The presidents of both houses were chosen by the Head of State. Constitutionally, Louis Napoleon could hardly have been in a stronger position.

Following the adoption of the new constitution, legislative elections were set for 29 February and 1 March 1852. Persigny, as Minister of the Interior, used all the means at his disposal to obtain results favourable to the regime. Certain candidates were designated as the 'official' choice of the administration, which lent them its powerful support while blatantly discriminatory against their opponents. In such circumstances – and with martial law still in force in some regions – it is scarcely surprising that the elections produced a sweeping victory for the Bonapartists, who polled 5.2 million votes to fewer than 1 million for the opposition. In only three cases was an official candidate defeated (all in western strongholds of Legitimism), and out of 265 deputies only seven coud be reckoned as opponents of Louis Napoleon. Only three of these seven were republicans, one of whom defected to the regime, while the other two refused to swear the oath required to allow them to take their seats. Louis Napoleon could not have wished for a more sympathetic Legislative Body, though it is worth noting that abstentions from voting were high: 37 per cent on average, with much higher proportions in some of the larger cities, such as Marseille (55 per cent) and Saint-Etienne (75 per cent).[13]

The Prince President revelled in his untramelled power, especially in the period before the new legislature first met in March 1851. For two months, he was able to rule by decree, feverishly enacting some of the projects which had long been maturing in his mind. Presidential decrees extended the road and railway networks, provided for the development of canals, harbours and telegraph lines, discouraged foundry work, and tackled questions of public health and housing. More controversially, he confiscated the Orleanist estates, which Louis Philippe (with dubious legality) had transferred to his sons, and used the money to endow mutual aid societies and other charities. Orleanists were not alone in regarding this act as bizarre on the part of someone who claimed to be the champion of order and property against the depredations of socialists. Even some of Louis Napoleon's closest collaborators (Morny, Rouher, Fould) were alarmed, and temporarily resigned from his service. They need never have worried, for the President issued much more draconian decrees against the 'reds' than those directed against the house of Orleans. The National Guard was virtually abolished. Cafés and cabarets – often the breeding-grounds of republican dissent – were strictly licensed. The press was gagged.

All the signs pointed to a restoration sooner rather than later. The Civil Code was renamed the *Code Napoléon*: military standards once more bore the imperial eagle: the President took to appearing in full military uniform. By delaying, as F A Simpson suggests, Louis Napoleon was perhaps hoping to create the impression that the Republic had somehow died a natural death.[14] After another provincial tour in September 1852, he was convinced that the country was ready, all the more so in that his visit took him to the south and west, previously the regions which had expressed most opposition to the *coup d'état*, and where crowds now hailed him with cries of *Vive l'empereur!*. At a banquet held in his honour in Bordeaux on 9 October, for the first time he explicitly referred to the possibility of a restoration, which, he claimed, the French people in their great majority desired. Back in Paris, he immediately set preparations in motion to effect the change of regime. A plebiscite was held on 21/22 November to seek popular approval, which was obtained by a vote of almost 8 million to 0.25 million, with almost 2 million abstentions. Interestingly, although Louis Napoleon's overall majority was much the same as in the previous referendum, it revealed a certain evolution in the voting patterns. In the north-west and the centre of France, Louis lost votes to the conservatives (except in Brittany), whereas he made gains in the more liberal eastern regions. In other words, the plebiscite confirmed the triumph of a 'popular' Bonapartism. Among the sixteen departments which had given the *démoc-socs* an absolute majority of the votes in 1849, only one (the Cher) registered a slight diminution in the votes cast for Louis Napoleon between 1851 and 1852. In areas such as Champagne and Brittany, there was a close correlation between the vote for the extreme left in the local elections of August 1852 and the 'yes' votes in the plebiscite. In Reims it was the workers who petitioned for the return of the Empire while the middle classes remained cool. The Mediterranean south was the only area where left-wing opposition to the plebiscite existed on any substantial scale.[15] Thus it was amidst scenes of general joy and festivity that, on 2 December 1852, Louis Napoleon Bonaparte was proclaimed the Emperor Napoleon III and installed at the Tuileries. His faith in his destiny seemed to have been amply justified.

. . .

## NOTES AND REFERENCES

1. Typically disparaging are Barrot O 1878 *Mémoires posthumes*, 4 vols. For Montalembert's opinion, see Lecanuet R P 1895–1902 *Montalembert*, 3 vols, vol 2, p. 415
2. Persigny F duc de 1896 (2nd edn) *Mémoires*
3. Dansette A 1961 *Louis Napoléon à la conquête du pouvoir*
4. Hauterive E de 1925 *Napoléon III et le Prince Napoléon (Correspondance inédite)*, p. 53ff. Reproduced here as quoted by Thompson J M 1954 *Louis Napoleon and the Second Empire*, Blackwell, p. 61
5. Quoted by Dansette 1961, p. 277

6. Echard W E 1974 'Louis Napoleon and the French decision to intervene at Rome in 1849: a new appraisal', *Canadian Journal of History*, IX, Dec. 263–74

7. Jerrold B 1874–82 *The Life of Napoleon III*. Longman, 4 vols, vol 3, p. 79ff

8. Ibid., p. 96

9. Ibid., p. 110

10. Ibid., pp. 221–3

11. Hugo V 1877 *Histoire d'un crime*

12. Ménager B 1988 *Les Napoléons du peuple*, pp. 110ff

13. Ibid. and *Historical Dictionary of France from the 1815 Restoration to the Second Empire*, 2 vols 1987 ed Newman E L, Greenwood Press, vol 1, article, 'Elections'

14. Simpson F A 1960 *Louis Napoleon and the Recovery of France*. Longman, pp. 190–91

15. Ménager 1988 pp. 15–17

# Chapter 5

# MASTER OF FRANCE
# (1852–1863)?

Having re-established the dynasty, Napoleon III was faced with the problem of how to perpetuate it. That meant, in the first place, providing it with an heir. As President, he had not felt confident enough about his future to marry, and had sought consolation in the arms of Miss Howard. She, however, was deemed an unsuitable consort for an emperor, and was hastily pensioned off with a title and a generous allowance. Princess Mathilde, wooed in vain in 1836, once again became the object of Napoleon's suit, but she continued to decline his advances. A number of foreign princesses likewise turned him down. In January 1853 his luck changed. Having made the acquaintance of Eugénie de Montijo, a beautiful Spanish noblewoman, he rapidly became engaged to her and then married her on 6 February 1853. The Emperor's choice of spouse was not at all to the liking of his counsellors, who would have preferred a judicious alliance with one of Europe's royal houses, but he justified it as a love match. In the long run, it was to prove a far from ideal partnership from either a personal or a political point of view. In the short term, while emphasising the *parvenu* aspect of the regime, it met Napoleon's need for a wife and also provided beauty, brilliance and flair at court to enhance the prestige of the Empire. When, in 1856, Eugénie gave birth to a son, Eugène Louis, the Prince Imperial, the future of the dynasty began to look more secure.

· · ·

## THE LIMITS OF AUTHORITARIANISM

The Empire was established, but how much power had the Emperor? Conventional wisdom has it that Napoleon's reign can be divided into two phases, one 'authoritarian', the other 'liberal', the dividing line being located in 1860. The traditional picture is misleading in a number of respects. First, there is the matter of chronology: the 'liberal empire' was only established in 1870. Second, and more importantly, the conventional wisdom implies a radical transformation in the character of the regime and in the outlook of the Emperor, neither of which took place. Certainly, the Empire evolved – but there was also a good deal of continuity. Napoleon III, from beginning to end, remained neither a traditional conservative, committed to the defence of the status quo, nor an orthodox liberal, convinced of the necessity of a parliamentary regime, but a *politique*, a political operator, who over the course of eighteen years – a long time in politics – manoeuvred with immense skill to maintain himself in power and to retain the political initiative in the face of all the vicissitudes of fortune. Until the calamity of military defeat in 1870, Napoleon III proved himself to be a survivor, adept in adjusting to the shifting balance of political forces in the country. Before it was either 'authoritarian' or 'liberal', the Empire was a 'personalist' regime. At its centre was a lonely figure, wielding power through men who often did not share his vision of politics. By nature an idealist, Napoleon III was by necessity an opportunist, battling against long odds to found a dynasty and to shape events in conformity with his convictions.

For Napoleon had not sought power merely to enjoy the trappings of high office. The author of *Napoleonic Ideas* believed that it was the duty of government to govern, and he intended to rule as well as reign. From the outset, it was understood that his would be the hand which guided the destiny of the French state. He had ministers to advise him, but they were responsible to him alone: there was no constitutional provision for a council of ministers. Napoleon III received his ministers individually, and discussed policy with them *tête-à-tête*. Twice a week they were convoked for a meeting which the Emperor chaired and which discussed an agenda drawn up by him. Napoleon tended to listen, rather than to speak, but final decisions were always taken by him, alone.[1] The idea that he was too ignorant or too idle to grasp the details of policy is entirely mythical, belied by his many annotations of ministerial papers.[2]

But it was one thing for the Emperor to decide policy, another to have it implemented. Napoleon III was too dependent on the good will of numerous individuals and on the smooth running of the machinery of government to be in a position to wield absolute power. Even the hand-picked ministerial team did not comprise a collection of docile, subservient 'creatures' of the Emperor, but men of stature, neither easily ignored nor replaced. A number came from the world of Orleanism and retained their links with the *notables*. Such, for instance, were Fould, Minister of State and later Finance Minister; the Corsican Abbatucci, Minister of Justice; and Foreign Minister Drouyn de Lhuys. Three of the most important ministers (Baroche, Billault and Rouher) came from humbler backgrounds originally, but were also Orleanist in outlook, while Morny, the Emperor's half-brother, epitomised the imperial regime's connections with big business. Only Persigny, Minister of the Interior and long-time fellow conspirator with the young Louis Napoleon, could be counted a genuine Bonapartist among the Emperor's top advisers, apart from members of his family, such as the ex-tremely anticlerical, self-proclaimed 'left' Bonapartist, Prince Jerome Napoleon, nicknamed 'Plon-Plon', the Emperor's temperamental cousin, and Walewski, the illegitimate son of Napoleon I. Hence the much-quoted *mot* attributed to Napoleon III: 'What a government is mine! The empress is a legitimist: Napoléon-Jérôme a republican: Morny Orleanist, I myself am a socialist. The only Bonapartist is Persigny, and he is mad.'[3]

Napoleon needed support also from the personnel of the regime's political and administrative institutions. The senators posed few problems, since appointment to the Senate was made chiefly as a reward for services rendered to the Empire (usually to army officers and former ministers and bureaucrats). The Legislative Body, however, proved to be less docile, despite the attempt to pack the house with 'official' candidates. Govern-ment intervention in elections undoubtedly ensured a certain continuity and stability of personnel in parliament over the period 1852–69, but the great majority of deputies continued to be rich *notables* who would have been perfectly at home in the Assembly of the July Monarchy. Almost a quarter were mem-bers of the industrial and financial elite, including such as the ironmasters Wendel and Schneider. About a fifth were landed proprietors, wealthy enough to live as *rentiers*. Another quarter were former bureaucrats. As in the ministerial team, devotees of Orleanism were more in evidence than genuine Bonapartists. They were men who, having rallied to the Empire out of fear of disorder, were always likely to look for an enlargement of the limited political role assigned to them by the constitution once the 'red menace' had receded. Evolution of the regime towards a more liberal, parliamentary model of government was always a likely consequence of the establishment of prosperity and stability.[4] Paradoxically, the very successes of the Empire undermined the conditions favourable to authoritarianism. Even in the earliest days, Napoleon realised that, as a mouthpiece for the opinions of the notables, the Legislative Body was not to be treated as a cipher. Indeed, the business of choosing 'official' candidates from among the local *notables* was itself a delicate issue, capable of alienating unsuccessful contenders.[5] How to mobilise and to retain the support of the old ruling elites remained a perennial problem for Napoleon III.

His hope had been that, by emasculating parliament, he could clear the way for direct administrative rule. The *conseil d'état* was seen by many contemporaries as the nerve-centre of the new regime, while the prefects were widely regarded as despots in their own departments. In practice, however, the Second Empire was far from being the purely *état administratif* that republican propaganda made it out to be, let alone the harbinger of twentieth-century totalitarianism that some modern historians have discerned. The *conseil d'état* never enjoyed the pre-eminent role in the making of law that was originally intended for it in the constitution. On the one hand, its ability to thwart the policies of ministers was limited, given that the latter could always claim to have the backing of the Emperor. On the other hand, Napoleon himself was never in a position to coerce the *conseil*, which frequently blocked or sabotaged imperial legislative projects. Recruited essentially from the ranks of the professional bourgeoisie, the *conseillers*, even more than the ministers, numbered few genuine Bonapartists and were predominantly Orleanist in outlook. Their loyalty to the Empire was by no means unconditional. Napoleon III could with some justification blame his failure to do more for the working classes on their innate conservatism.[6]

Nor were the prefects the corrupt and cynical agents of bureaucratic despotism who loomed so large in republican demonology. Certainly, more than ever they were confirmed in their role as the key link between the central government and the people, responsible for the implementation of government policy and for building up local support. Upper-class (frequently aristocratic) in social origin, highly educated and generally devoted to the ideal of serving the state, prefects were almost invariably loyal to their master whatever their own personal political preferences, but they were by no means a homogeneous body. Some were old-style conservatives, hostile to change and to democracy, and keen to cultivate the traditional elites. Others were of the centre-right, socially conservative but not opposed to the advent of manhood suffrage. A third group could be described as 'authoritarian democrats', anti-clerical and committed to the implementation of social and economic change by means of the apparatus of the state, while a fourth category included those who wished for political as well as social and economic change in order to break the power of the old *notables*. The last group, the most dedicated to 'Napoleonic ideas', was also the smallest and the least successful, especially when, like Bérard in the Isère, they ran into resolute opposition from the local elite. More effective were the 'authoritarian democrats' – men like Janvier de la Motte in the Eure – who combined their appeal to the masses with skilful cultivation of the *notables*. Legitimist and Orleanist prefects were appointed to run overtly conservative departments. Thus, most prefects failed to monopolise patronage and political influence and constantly found themselves obliged to compromise with local *notables* who, through their dominance of the *conseils généraux* (local assemblies theoretically subject to the authority of the prefect), were well placed to air their views. Deputies, too, and even mayors often conspired to undermine prefectoral authority. Little wonder, then, that in the end the majority opted for a non-political role, preferring to cultivate the image of disinterested civil servant rather than that of Bonapartist *gauleiter*.[7]

Given the political and administrative machinery of the Empire, Napoleon III was therefore in no position to rule as a despot, enlightened or otherwise. His unwillingness to contemplate the creation of a one-party state acted as another limitation on his power. Napoleon wanted to be a truly 'national' head of state, Emperor of all the French. Instinctively, he tried to conciliate opponents rather than to crush them: hence the series of amnesties which he declared throughout the 1850s, culminating in the general amnesty of 1859. The Second Empire was not a police state – at least, no more of a police state than the Second or Third Republics.[8] True, in 1852 Napoleon had tried to establish a new Ministry of Police under Maupas, which reflected his interest in having direct control over the police. This, however, had been a short-lived experiment which had succumbed to the machinations of its rivals at the Ministry of the Interior and the Ministry of War. Rather than anticipating twentieth-century models of repression, the political police of the Second Empire drew upon existing administrative regulations.

Nor can Napoleon be considered essentially as a 'man on horseback', a kind of Latin-American style military dictator. The army, of course, had carried out the *coup d'état* on the new Emperor's behalf, and inevitably it occupied a special place in his affections, benefiting from many tokens of his esteem. A new Military Medal was devised, and its recipients entitled also to a small pension. Non-commissioned officers were awarded pay rises. The Imperial Guard was reconstituted. In general, the army was perceived to loom larger in national life, its status highlighted as much by the military parades and ceremonies that were a central feature of the *fête impériale* as by the wars, both European and colonial, undertaken by the regime. The army, however, neither ruled nor sought to turn the Empire into a military dictatorship. By the 1860s, it contained elements willing to vote against the Emperor and in September 1870 it offered no resistance to the overthrow of Napoleon.[9]

Republicans depicted the Empire as 'clericalist', but the Church was never a completely reliable pillar of the regime. In the 1850s, certainly, Napoleon III went out of his way to cultivate its support. Parish priests, like soldiers, were paid more, which encouraged vocations. Church schools – notably those run by female religious orders – expanded dramatically. Napoleon's role in the restoration of Pius IX to the throne of Peter in 1849 was also remembered with gratitude by churchmen and Catholic voters. Even the 'liberal' Catholic leader Charles de Montalembert at first accepted the necessity of the *coup d'état* and agreed to run for the Legislative Body as an 'official' candidate.[10] He was, however, soon disillusioned with the regime and emerged as the lone voice of opposition in the legislature of 1852 after penning a brochure, *Catholic Interests in the Nineteenth Century*, which denounced absolute power as the enemy of spiritual as much as of political freedom.[11] Few of his co-religionists agreed with him – certainly not the combative journalist Louis Veuillot, a far more representative voice of mid-nineteenth-century French Catholicism. His newspaper, *L'Univers*, was the favourite reading of the parish priests and championed an aggressive and ultramontane Catholicism that enjoyed widespread popularity among the faithful.[12]

On the other hand, Catholic leaders did not delude themselves that Napoleon III was genuinely attached to religious ideals. He consistently turned a deaf ear to their calls for the repeal of the Organic Articles, the series of controls and regulations permitted to the state in Church affairs introduced by the first Napoleon. Though willing to sack a number of prominent anticlerical academics, the Emperor resisted the demand for 'freedom of higher education', which would have involved the establishment of Catholic universities and an end to the state monopoly. The bishops, in their great majority, publicly supported the regime (though there were some unreconstructed legitimists like Monseigneur Pie of Poitiers), but Napoleon, for his part, was all too well aware that their goodwill was conditional, dependent, above all, on his own continuing commitment to the interests of the papacy. Napoleon III's sympathies for the cause of Italian nationalism were incompatible with the maintenance of the temporal power of the Pope and, with the Italian war of 1859, *L'Univers* had no hesitation in affirming that its devotion to God took precedence over its loyalty to Caesar. The Church was not a reliable instrument for the dissemination of 'Napoleonic ideas'.[13]

From the outset, therefore, Napoleon III governed with many constraints imposed on his power. The conservative bias of the regime was unmistakable, but it was by no means as authoritarian as the Emperor would have preferred or as his opponents alleged. That is not to say that one should minimise its capacity for repression. Napoleon had already demonstrated his ruthlessness in carrying out the *coup d'état*, and throughout the 1850s the police continued to crack down on republican opponents of the regime. More than 300 arrests were made between 1853 and 1859 for alleged membership of secret societies. In January 1858, in the aftermath of a serious attempt on his life by the Italian conspirator Orsini, Napoleon ordered draconian measures to be taken against the fomentors of discord. As he told the Legislative Body, the real danger to the country resided not in the allegedly excessive powers of the executive but in the absence of repressive laws with which to combat extremists.[14]

Recourse was again had to the army. The country was divided into five military districts, each headed by a marshal of

France, who was to ensure order in his area. In February, Minister of the Interior Billault prepared a law of 'general security', empowering the ministry to deport to Algeria or to Cayenne any person who had previously been convicted of participation in the June Days of 1848 or in resistance to the *coup d'état* of 1851, should this be deemed necessary in the interests of national security. On Napoleon's orders, the law was then applied in rigorous fashion by General Espinasse, who took over as Minister of the Interior and of General Security. Each prefect was instructed to make a certain number of arrests in his department, with the highest quotas fixed for those departments known to be sympathetic to republicanism. Under the vicious 'law of suspects', some 430 people were the victims of arbitrary arrest, most of them deported to Algeria. In 1858, the Second Empire's reputation for repression was well merited.

· · · ·

## THE CONSOLIDATION OF THE REGIME

Repression alone did not account for the consolidation of the regime. Propaganda also played its part. In the absence of modern techniques of communication, Napoleon's success was necessarily limited, but he can be said to have made the most of the means at his disposal.

Official tours of the provinces were one means of broadening his appeal. Thus, in 1858, he toured the west with the explicit aim of wooing the rural masses away from Legitimism. Well-informed as to the electoral geography of his support, he preferred to tour not those areas where his support was strong (like the Limousin and the Charente), but departments (like those in eastern France) where the popular milieux were tempted by republicanism. Workers were always carefully cultivated, as when, in 1852, the Emperor rewarded the 'most deserving' miners of Saint-Etienne with the Legion of Honour. (As we shall see, the response of the workers to the regime was mixed. Some, certainly, were won over, not least because of the military successes in the Crimea and in Italy. The annexation of Nice and Savoy, in particular, appealed to a strongly rooted popular chauvinism, nowhere more so than in the frontier areas.) Before illness put a stop to the tours, Napoleon was prepared to take to the road for a period of roughly three weeks, during which time he would be at the centre of all kinds of ceremonial, speechifying and popular festivity.[15]

Indeed, Napoleon III appreciated that holidays and festivals could be turned to political ends. The *fête impériale*, the extravagant round of balls, receptions and display, orchestrated in Paris by Eugénie and the court, and animated in the provinces by the prefects, was designed not merely to provide a good time for the favoured few, but rather to bring glamour and colour into the lives of the masses. Official celebrations, such as those surrounding the birth of the Prince Imperial in 1856, were turned into occasions of general rejoicing and merry-making. The birthday of Napoleon I, 15 August, was proclaimed a national holiday, the equivalent of what 14 July came to represent under the Third Republic. The criticism directed at the luxury and indulgence of the Empire by sober republicans may well reflect more than a puritanical distaste for excess. It could also be an acknowledgement that the festive side of the regime served to strengthen its popular appeal.

So, too, did the printed word, especially in the form of popular literature, such as the almanac. Items like the *Almanach de Napoléon*, distributed by itinerant hawkers, became important elements in the endeavours of the administration to nourish a popular Bonapartism.[16] Popular songs celebrating the Emperor were also widely diffused with official backing. Images of the imperial family were another time-honoured device for penetrating popular culture, and the regime promoted the acquisition of representations of the sovereign and of members of the imperial family. Other images recalled the military triumphs of the first Napoleon, and, of course, celebrated those of Napoleon III. Sometimes they simply glorified the army, in an effort to harness nationalism to Bonapartism. Pro-Bonapartist newspapers were founded, such as *L'Opinion Nationale* (1861), while the government also subsidised other, ostensibly apolitical, organs such as *Le Moniteur du Soir*. Probably more influential than newspapers was the reproduction of official speeches, extracts from *L'Extinction du paupérisme*, and the texts of decrees likely to appeal to the *classes populaires*, such as amnesties. Altogether, official and unofficial propagandists for the regime sought to put across the message that Napoleon III was a wise and powerful sovereign, deeply solicitous for the welfare of his people.

The claim was not entirely without foundation. When a natural disaster occurred, like the terrible floods which covered the valleys of the Saône, the Rhône and the Loire in 1856, the Emperor made highly publicised visits to the scene of the disaster. Likewise, the regime strove to mitigate the effects of bad harvests in the mid 1850s. In the aftermath of the *coup d'état*, Napoleon was portrayed as the 'saviour of society', but as the economy recovered he was assigned the credit for the return of national prosperity.

Ultimately, however, the popular appeal of the Second Empire derived less from propaganda than from its novel blend of democracy and state control, which in the longer run served to emancipate the rural masses from their dependence on the *notables* in their region.[17] The advent of universal male suffrage may not have ended the traditional domination of the old elites right away, but it certainly contributed to the politicisation of the countryside and allowed peasants to begin to think of themselves as having a permanent say in the political process. Centralisation was an even more important weapon in the war against the power of the local *notables*. The state subsidised the services of France's 36,000 impoverished communes, and, as the source of favours, was able to demand loyalty in return. Local government was, in effect, an extension of central government. Villages elected their own municipal councils, but these had only very limited powers under the Second Empire. The mayor himself was appointed by the state, and was as much its representative as that of the commune. He was a crucial figure in the politics of patronage, dispensing – or withholding-favours in accordance with support for the regime. His business was to deliver the vote of his village for the official candidate, and to convey the message that failure on his part would mean an end to state subsidies. The mayor was thus the key election agent of the Bonapartist party. Bonapartism flourished by building up a clientele at the level of the commune. Where the system worked well, dependence on the benefactions of the local *notables* was removed. True, as we have seen, prefects (the chief exponents of the politics of clientelism in their departments) often had to proceed with caution in the face of opposition from the local elites, but an undeniable democratisation of politics took place under the Empire. Ironically, because of the demise of the Empire in 1870, it was the republicans rather than the Bonapartists who were to reap most of the benefits.

In the shorter term, the impact of the new style of politics could be measured to some degree in the continuing electoral success of the regime. In 1857, the 'official' candidates polled 89 per cent of the vote, even if the turnout was low (60 per cent). The Empire seemed set to endure, and not solely because of the efficacy of repression and authoritarian rule. By 1860, in the aftermath of success in the Italian war, Napoleon III was at the height of his power and closest to realising the Bonapartist dream of achieving a new kind of political consensus. Even so, the spectre of opposition continued to haunt him.

· · ·

## THE SURVIVAL OF OPPOSITION

It is a mistake to think of the period 1852–60 as the 'silent years', a time when all opposition lay crushed under the weight of authoritarian rule. In the first place, conservative opposition had not entirely died out. The most intransigent Legitimists, following the instructions of their pretender, the comte de Chambord, withdrew altogether from politics, but others such as Berryer and Falloux continued to be politically active, sometimes joining forces with the more conservative of the Orleanists. In Legitimist bastions of the west and south-west, noble landowners could still exercise sway at the local level. Elsewhere, in the department of the Nord, for instance, Legitimists controlled the Society of Saint-Vincent de Paul, a Catholic charity founded to assist the poor, but suspected by the government of being a front for the extension of Legitimist influence. Moreover, as religion came to be the banner to which Legitimists increasingly rallied, the split between the Empire and the Church after the Italian war of 1859 furnished them with ample opportunities to attack the regime.

Orleanist liberals continued to hanker after the restoration of a parliamentary system of government, and used newspapers such as the *Journal des Débats* and the *Revue des Deux Mondes* to air implicit criticisms of the regime. Others expressed their distaste in speeches at the Bar and in elections to the French Academy (membership of which was coveted by Napoleon).[18] Learned historical and philosophical works sometimes made allusions to the contemporary situation which were not lost on the educated public. Liberal Catholics, led by Montalembert, refused their support. None of this opposition, it is true, carried any weight with the majority of the population, and it also has to be set against the large numbers of former Orleanists who rallied to the regime. Nevertheless, Napoleon III had not succeeded, as he had hoped, in eliminating all loyalties to previous regimes, and among disappointed aspirants to official candidatures he faced a new generation of discontented seekers after office.

Republican opposition was muted in the 1850s. The repression which followed the *coup d'état* had taken its toll, and many prominent republicans were either in gaol, or like Victor Hugo, in exile. The ban on republican organisations and the muzzling of the press prevented the formation of any overt or sustained opposition. Nevertheless, the basis of a republican movement survived underground. In Paris and Lyon there were many artisans and writers who remained loyal to the republican idea. Students, too, frequently harboured republican sympathies, as did disaffected bourgeois (often lawyers) who, when the time was right, could emerge as leaders of the republican cause. Clandestine meetings were held under cover of bar-room encounters, leisure activities and private gatherings, and proscribed literature, such as Hugo's *Les Châtiments*, was smuggled into the country and distributed. The funerals of republican activists provided occasions for more public demonstrations of opposition, and there were also isolated protests in the form of cries and banners to remind the police of the visceral hatred which most republicans felt towards the regime.

The legislative elections of June 1857 permitted republican contestation of the regime to come to the surface, at least in the cities, even if, as a result of the 'official candidate' system and the intimidation of the electorate by the forces of order, a fair fight was never in prospect. The opposition was prevented from organising a genuine campaign, which once again allowed the government to register a resounding victory at the polls. In a 65 per cent turnout, official candidates won by 5.5 million votes to 665,000. Yet the outcome was not altogether reassuring from Napoleon III's point of view. Despite inroads made into the legitimist strongholds of the west, the empire still faced determined opposition, now readily identifiable as republican rather than conservative. Some 100 republican candidates had run for office, even if only six were successful (five in Paris and one in Lyon). Two of the Parisian republicans refused to take the oath and resigned their seats. A third, Cavaignac, died. In the subsequent by-elections of 1858, republicans won two of the three seats, thus creating the celebrated 'group of five' in the Legislative Body. Napoleon III was displeased, even alarmed. He had reason to be: the republican movement may still have been small and internally divided, but it was still alive, and had even re-emerged as a party.

· · · ·

## TOWARDS LIBERALISATION?

On 22 November 1860, Napoleon III startled his ministers by announcing that he planned to introduce a number of reforms. Almost all (Walewski was an exception) were horrified to discover that he intended a certain 'liberalisation' of the regime. Despite their objections, he pressed ahead, and on 24 November 1860 he issued decrees which allowed the legislature the right to reply to the annual message from the throne, to discuss bills and to propose amendments at the committee stage, and to permit publication of the debates. He also named three ministers without portfolio to defend government policy before the deputies. A subsequent measure, a *senatus-consultum* of 31 December 1861, gave parliament important controls over government expenditure, in particular the right to discuss the budget clause by clause.

Most historians agree that these initiatives were the work of the Emperor himself, a gesture from on high, made while Napoleon was as powerful as he ever had been or would be. They were not concessions wrung from him by a renascent opposition. The reforms, however, can still be seen as a response to one of the Empire's more serious weaknesses; namely, its failure to win over completely the old Orleanist elites, upon whose goodwill the regime depended so much for its smooth functioning. As the danger from the 'reds' receded, the Orleanists soon demonstrated that they had relinquished none of their aspirations to political pre-eminence within the framework of a liberal parliamentary system. Even before the issuing of the decrees of 24 November 1860, there had been signs that they were chafing under the restrictions imposed by the constitution. In the Legislative Body, they subjected each item of the budget to minute scrutiny, in effect finding pretexts for illegal interpellations of government policy. Baroche, at the time the only minister who had to stand up to questioning in the house, came under increasing pressure, while Morny, the president of the chamber, became increasingly convinced that the time had come to remove some of the more obvious sources of discontent among parliamentarians. As one who moved in Orleanist circles himself, Morny was well placed to judge the temper of the *notables*, and with his direct line to the Emperor he did not shrink from using his influence on their behalf. It was he and Walewski who persuaded Napoleon of the wisdom of taking the initiative in the matter of reforms, before a day dawned when they would be extorted from him. Napoleon III had no intention of restoring a parliamentary regime on the lines of the July Monarchy, but he was willing to experiment with measures which might secure the support of the Orleanist notables – all the more readily in that he was only granting formally rights which the chamber had already arrogated to itself in the course of 1860.

The new overtures had the effect of stimulating a revival of political life both inside and outside parliament. Expectations of further reforms were raised. The republican deputy Emile Ollivier was encouraged, and began the evolution that was to bring him to preside over the 'Liberal empire' in 1870. As he told Morny, the reforms of 1860, if they were a beginning, would guarantee the future of the Empire, but, if not, disaster would follow.[19] Both in the Chamber and in the Senate, the years 1861 and 1862 witnessed some remarkable debates, notably on Italian affairs and on the question of the temporal power of the papacy. The Emperor's three spokesmen in parliament, Billault, Baroche and Magne, found themselves stretched to defend the policies of their imperial master. In a situation where clerical and conservative spokesmen like Emile Keller appeared to be the most effective critics of the Empire, castigating its flirtations with the forces of revolution at home and abroad, it fell to Ollivier to defend Napoleon as the man who, alone, had known how to steer a prudent course between the excesses of revolution and reaction. On 14 March 1861, he declared that, should the Emperor go further down the path to liberty, republicans like himself would be able to rally to the regime.[20] In spite of Ollivier's best efforts, however, and much to the indignation of Persigny, now back at the Ministry of the Interior, Keller's clerical amendment still won some ninety-one votes. Persigny threatened to take his revenge at the elections of 1863.

That is not exactly what happened. The elections took place

on 30–31 May 1863 in an atmosphere of considerable excite-
ment. This time, the opposition as well as the government
conducted a strenuous campaign. Persigny instructed the prefects to place the full weight of the administration behind the
'official' candidates, 'so that the good faith of the people may
not be led astray by clever language or equivocal promises'.[21]
Support was withheld from some twenty-four of the ninety-one
'clerical' deputies who had been troublesome in 1861, and the
usual obstacles were placed in the way of opposition candidates:
threats to newspapers, prosecutions for peddling in response to
the distribution of handbills, gerrymandering of constituencies.
But the sheer number of opposition candidates made the 'official' candidate system increasingly unworkable, in the larger
cities especially. In the countryside, voting was less free, but
prefects in northern and central France realised that local
*notables*, stirred into opposition by the government's anticlerical
and free-trade policies, were not easily to be coerced when they
put themselves forward as the champions of local interests.

The results were a substantial blow to the government. True,
it polled 5.3 million votes (73 per cent of the votes cast) to the
opposition's 1.9 million (27 per cent), winning 250 seats against
thirty-two. Polling, however, had been heavier than in 1852 and
1857, and it was evident that many voters who had formerly
abstained were now prepared to side with the opposition.
Whereas rural France, on the whole, remained loyal to the
Empire (with further gains to the regime in the west), urban
France returned a massive vote of no confidence. In Paris, no
government candidate was elected: of the nine Parisian deputies, eight were republican and the other was the veteran
Orleanist politician Thiers. The results were comparable in all
the other main cities – Marseille, Lyon, Lille, Bordeaux,
Toulouse. In all, there were now seventeen republican deputies
in the chamber, plus fifteen 'independents', mainly Catholics or
monarchists who, however conservative, refused to be numbered
among the Empire's adherents. Persigny tried to put a brave
face on the outcome, representing it as a triumph. But everyone
– the Emperor included – knew that it was a moral defeat.
Napoleon did not hesitate to sack his old comrade for having
mismanaged the campaign, though he did make him a duke for
his loyalty over the years.

Morny advised Napoleon that, in the light of the election
results, further liberalisation of the Empire was both desirable

and inevitable. The Emperor ignored the advice. Napoleon had no intentions of allowing the Empire to be transformed into a constitutional regime under which Morny would be prime minister. Such concessions as he was prepared to make to liberalism were mere window dressing, calculated manoeuvres in his eternal balancing act, as he sought to win 'left' support for his Italian policies to compensate for his provocations to the conservatives. Yet he was not ready to break completely with the latter, by abandoning the papacy and siding openly with the Italian revolutionaries who wanted to make Rome their capital, if necessary by force. Hence his dismissal of the pro-Italian Thouvenel from the Quai d'Orsay and the recall of Drouyn in the run-up to the elections. That move, at least, produced the desired effect, since the results were a severe disappointment to hardline 'clericals', in that some of the most prominent Catholic spokesmen (Keller, Montalembert, Cochin) were defeated, and, more importantly, the Roman question was shown to be an issue of profound indifference to the French masses.[22] On the morrow of the elections, a renewed challenge from the left may have been inescapable, but Napoleon's initial reaction was to get tough rather than to bow to pressure. As a sop to liberal opinion, he brought the anticlerical historian Victor Duruy into his government team at the Ministry of Education, but his principal response was to appoint Billault, then, on his sudden death, Rouher, as Minister of State to cope with the parliamentary opposition. Rouher, a lawyer with an immense capacity for hard work and a formidable debater, was an unabashed apologist for the 'authoritarian' Empire. He it was who increasingly established the governmental tone, rejecting the call of Thiers, in January 1864, for 'the necessary freedoms' (by which he meant individual freedom, freedom of the press, free elections and ministerial responsibility within a genuinely parliamentary system). In 1864, Napoleon III might be willing to try to cultivate the support of workers by permitting them the legal right to strike, but he refused to contemplate further concessions to parliamentary liberalism. These would come only in 1867, after Napoleon's position had deteriorated as a result of dramatic changes on the international scene.

. . .

## THE EMPEROR'S HEALTH

If, after 1860, Napoleon III began to appear as something less than an all-powerful ruler, this was not entirely attributable to the rise of political opposition. It was also because he increasingly experienced problems with his health.[23] Physical weakness exacerbated his propensity to hesitation when confronted with the need to take decisive action. After the age of fifty, he had aged rapidly, greying, growing fatter and suffering from gout. Already in the mid-1850s his health had given cause for concern, to the point where his old friend and physician Dr Conneau had recommended calling in Dr Robert Ferguson from London for advice. On 6 May 1856, Ferguson diagnosed nervous exhaustion, one symptom of which was a loss of sexual desire and potency (not problems conventionally associated with a sovereign notorious for his marital infidelities). In keeping with his notion of patriotism if not with medical ethics, Ferguson informed the British Foreign Office of how he had found the Emperor's medical condition, and in consequence Foreign Minister Lord Clarendon wrote to ambassador Cowley in Paris to warn him that he could expect sudden changes in the Emperor's character in the foreseeable future: 'Apathy, irritation, caprice, infirmity of purpose are upon the cards, as the result of an exhausted nervous system and diseased organs, which ensue from such exhaustion. The political results of this may be fearful.'[24]

Ferguson's remedy was rest, a change of diet and taking the waters at a spa resort (which is how Napoleon acquired the habit of going to Plombières in the summer). Thereafter, despite an apparent recovery of his sexual appetite, he was subject to bouts of illness and depression. In May 1861, he complained of severe pains in his legs, all the more alarming because his doctors seemed unable to diagnose their cause. Conneau recommended trying the waters of Vichy rather than those of Plombières, which he did from 1861 to 1864. In October 1863, he had a fainting spell at Biarritz, followed by a second in August 1864 (brought on by a session with his then mistress, Marguerite Bellanger). From 1863, he suffered from urinary difficulties, which may have been the result of gravel or the development of a stone in the bladder. The latter was finally diagnosed in August 1865, but Napoleon refused to have it treated because of his desire not to be away from the political scene. By 1866, rumours abounded that his health was on the point of collapse. Certainly, by then, his appearance – portly, puffy, lame – did not inspire confidence.

It would, however, be wrong to exaggerate the extent of Napoleon's physical decline after 1860. Victor Duruy, for one, remembered him as still a masterful ruler at the time of his own ministerial appointment.[25] What is true is that the Emperor decided to relax some of his earlier tight control over domestic policy for personal reasons. These had to do with more than the state of his health. Easily bored with the routine business of government, Napoleon was also eager to return to some of the scholarly pursuits of his youth. From 1860, he had been planning a *Life of Julius Caesar*, which he began to research seriously in 1861, calling on the assistance of helpers and experts directed by Alfred Maury, whom he appointed librarian at the Tuileries. Hortense Cornu, his long-estranged childhood friend, was reconciled to him at this time, and again acted as research assistant as she had done while he was a prisoner at Ham. By March 1862, having frequently neglected state business to apply himself to his studies, Napoleon had produced a first draft (the text having been dictated to and corrected by his secretary Mocquard). He then invited Victor Duruy to produce a forthright critique. The work finally appeared in two volumes in 1865–66. Though not entirely bereft of scholarly merit, it was intended primarily as a demonstration of the 'great man' theory of history already set out in *Des idées napoléoniennes*. Its purpose was avowedly apologetic, nowhere more so than when he tried to justify the *coup d'état* of the 2 December by presenting Caesar as a man driven to similar action by party strife and disorder in the Republic. In similar vein, opponents of the regime seized the opportunity to criticise 'Caesarism' under the pretext of writing reviews of the book. The 'immortals' of the French Academy, true to their Orleanist leanings, took pleasure in denying him the membership which he hoped the *Life* might bring him.[26]

Napoleon, however, had by no means abandoned himself to writing history rather than making it. He still aspired to the role of leading world statesman. He was not fully master of France, but he dreamed of being arbiter of the destiny of Europe. There, too, disappointment lay in store for him.

## NOTES AND REFERENCES

1. Insights into Napoleon III's style of government may be derived from the memoirs of his ministers, eg *Journal d'Hippolyte Fortoul, ministre de l'Instruction Publique et des cultes (1811–1856), vol I, 1er janvier–30 juin 1855* (ed) Massa-Gille G 1979, Droz: Duruy V 1901 *Notes et souvenirs*, 2 vols
2. Smith W H C 1982 *Napoléon III*, pp. 175–76
3. The quotation is cited by almost all biographers of Napoleon III, in slightly different forms: cf. Jerrold B 1882 *The Life of Napoleon III*. Longman vol 4, p. 378
4. Plessis A 1985 *Rise and Fall of the Second Empire 1852–1871*. (French edn, 1979) Cambridge University Press
5. Zeldin T 1958 *The Political System of Napoleon III*. Macmillan
6. Wright V 1972 *Le Conseil d'Etat sous le Second Empire*.
7. Le Clère B and Wright V 1973 *Les préfets du Second Empire*.
8. Payne H C 1965 *The Police State of Louis Napoleon Bonaparte 1851–1860*. University of Washington Press
9. On the army, see Serman W 1982 *Les Officiers français dans la nation 1848–1870*, and Holmes R 1984 *The Road to Sedan: the French Army 1866–1870*. Royal Historical Society
10. Lecanuet 1895–1902 *Montalembert*, vol 3, p. 38
11. Montalembert C de 1852 *Des intérêts catholiques au dix-neuvième siècle*.
12. Cf. Brown M L 1977 *Louis Veuillot, French Ultramontane Catholic, Journalist and Layman*. Moore (Durham, N C)
13. Maurain J 1930 *La politique ecclésiastique du Second Empire de 1852 à 1869* is the definitive study
14. Edleston R H 1931 *Napoleon III: Speeches from the Throne*. R I Severs, p. 149
15. Ménager B 1988 *Les Napoléons du peuple*, p. 121ff
16. Ibid., pp. 134–45
17. On this see Zeldin 1958 and Zeldin T 1973 *France 1848–1945*, vol 1, ch. on 'Bonapartism'
18. Reicher R 1963 'Anti-Bonapartist elections to the Académie Française during the Second Empire', *Journal of Modern History* pp. 33–45
19. Ollivier E 1895–1918 *L'Empire libéral: études, récits, souvenirs*, vol 5, p. 95
20. Ibid., pp. 141ff

21. Case L 1954 *French Opinion on War and Diplomacy during the Second Empire*, University of Pennsylvania Press, p. 155
22. Ibid., p. 159; Maurain 1930, pp. 634–67
23. Williams R 1971 *The Mortal Napoleon III*. Princeton University Press
24. Ibid., p. 61
25. Duruy 1901, vol 1, p. 183
26. See Kranzberg M 'An emperor writes history: Napoleon III's *Histoire de Jules César*', in Hughes H S (ed) 1954 *Teachers of History: Essays in Honor of Lawrence Bradford Packard*. Cornell University Press

## Chapter 6

# ARBITER OF EUROPE
## (1852–63)?

Many historians, following F A Simpson, see the Second Empire as a second Napoleonic age, a time when France regained the diplomatic initiative and Napoleon III, for a decade at least, made himself arbiter of Europe's destiny.[1] This view is not wrong in drawing attention to Napoleon's claims to be regarded as the leading European statesman of his era, but it exaggerates his ability to dictate personally the terms of international diplomacy. The Emperor gave new drive and direction to French foreign policy, creating all kinds of tensions and problems for those charged with the conduct of foreign relations in other countries, but he was never in any position to refashion the international order in conformity with his 'Napoleonic ideas'. As at home, so abroad, he appreciated better than anyone that there were strict limits to his power. Once again, his achievement was that of a political conjuror, dazzling others into thinking, mistakenly, that both he and his country were more powerful than they were in reality. Moreover, always a gambler, he enjoyed more than his share of good luck in his early years in power. His reputation as an adventurous maverick on the diplomatic scene was well merited, but his omnipotence was an illusion.

One point should be clarified. In keeping with his intention of making foreign policy his special domain, Napoleon had frequent recourse to secret diplomacy, bypassing the official Foreign Office personnel and machinery. These procedures have often been deplored as signs of the Emperor's inability to shake off his old conspiratorial ways. That is only partly true. Such strictures overlook the opposition which he encountered to his personal designs in foreign policy. As Foreign Minister, neither Drouyn de Lhuys nor Walewski shared his views, being

73

both partisans of good relations with Austria, the one country for which the Emperor seems to have had a deep-seated dislike. If Napoleon resorted to clandestine diplomacy, it was not simply because of a temperament innately inclined to conspiracy, and an attachment to his fellow-travelling Carbonarist past, but also because of a determination to pursue his own policies.

. . .

## REVISION

'The empire means peace.' So Louis Napoleon announced to the audience of businessmen who entertained him at Bordeaux on 9 October 1852, a month before the proclamation of the Empire. In the chancelleries of Europe, however, no one believed that the return of a Bonaparte to the throne of France boded well for peace. In his years in the political wilderness, Louis Napoleon had made no secret of his ambition to seek revision of the diplomatic order established by the treaties of 1814–15. In *Des idées napoléoniennes* he had spoken of the need to turn away from a Europe based on a 'Holy Alliance' of monarchs towards a Europe united on the basis of peoples and nationalities. His *politique des nationalités* aimed at the creation of a greater European confederation which satisfied dreams of national unification and at the same time guaranteed peace by promoting cooperation among the larger nation states. Conservatives at home and abroad feared that the advent of the Empire would launch France on a new and dangerous course in foreign policy. Tsar Nicholas I conveyed his disapproval by refusing to recognise Napoleon III as a brother monarch, entitled to address him as 'Monsieur mon frère'. (Told that he had to call the Tsar 'mon cher ami', Napoleon joked that he preferred to be known as a friend, since a man could choose his friends but not the members of his own family.)

Far from being recklessly innovative and hopelessly idealistic, Napoleon III's *politique des nationalités* was not a particularly original vision of international politics, since it embraced the aspirations of the entire French left at the time. Nor, in any case, did he pursue a *politique des nationalités* to the exclusion of all other concerns. His prime consideration was always French interests, as he understood them. 'Revision' was not fuelled solely by 'Napoleonic ideas'. All French governments since 1815

74

had resented the Vienna settlement and had sought to undermine the treaties in different ways. A criticism of the July
Monarchy had been that its foreign policy had not been vigorous enough. Napoleon III was therefore aware that he was
expected to conduct a more active and successful foreign policy
in order to reaffirm French prestige. The memory of Waterloo
had to be effaced, the map of Europe redrawn, French influence
reasserted. The cult of *la gloire* demanded nothing less, of a
Bonaparte above all. Napoleon knew also that success abroad
was vital to the consolidation of the dynasty.

Thus, whereas his cousin Prince Napoleon advocated a
'revolutionary' foreign policy, in which France would be the
champion of all 'oppressed peoples' (Poles, Irish, Italians and
others), the Emperor remained more of a realist, weighing the
French and dynastic interests at stake in any given situation.
Revision was always on his agenda, but not at all costs. He was
determined that France should not again have to face the Waterloo coalition, and he was therefore prepared to pay a high price
to woo the British Foreign Office, which never shed its distrust
of his ultimate ambitions. To try to convince foreign statesmen of
his pacific intentions, he made himself the leading advocate
of 'concert' diplomacy; that is, of international congresses of the
great powers which, meeting 'in concert', would resolve international disputes round the conference table rather than on the
battlefield.[2] Negotiation, not war, was to be Napoleon's preferred means of bringing about change in the international
order. Recognising the need to conciliate other powers, he
constantly sought to cultivate their good will. His highly individual and more energetic approach to the conduct of French
foreign relations was grounded in a shrewd appraisal of the
constraints on French power and on his own authority. He
knew that he could never be the sole arbiter of Europe, any
more than he could be completely master in his own house.

Napoleon had already signalled his new activist approach to
foreign policy during his time as President of the Second
Republic. Apart from his intervention in the Roman question,
which has already been discussed, in January 1849 he sounded
Britain about the possibility of limiting naval expansion, and in
March the same year he suggested Franco-British sponsor-
ship of a European congress which would resolve disputes likely
to threaten the peace. Neither proposal found favour with
Palmerston. In October he managed to associate himself with

Britain in giving support to Turkey when the latter refused to extradite Polish and Hungarian refugees whose return was demanded by Austria and Russia. That did not prevent him, only a month later, from making overtures to the Tsar regarding the partition of Turkey in a deal involving French compensation on the Rhine. In 1850, he floated the idea of French annexation of the Palatinate to Prussia and Austria in return for a benevolent French attitude to their aggrandisement. After a brief rift with Britain over the Don Pacifico incident, he joined with Britain and Russia in upholding the rights of Denmark in Schleswig-Holstein, and he also expressed his opposition to the incorporation of Austria into a Greater Germany. In another dispute, that of the Latin monks in Bethlehem and their Orthodox brethren, over the issue of who should enjoy the guardianship of the Holy Places, his stance led him ultimately to war. As so many people had feared, the Empire did not mean peace after all.

· · ·

## THE CRIMEA

It is true that Napoleon III never intended to become involved in hostilities over what he dismissed as 'the foolish affair of the Holy Places'. Contemporaries, notably the British writer A W Kinglake, a man who, as a defeated rival in love had a personal animus against Napoleon, accused him of embarking on a war of conquest abroad in order to reconcile domestic opinion to his regime.[3] The charge is a distortion of the events which resulted in the outbreak of the Crimean War. France's right to act as the protector of Latin Christians in the Ottoman Empire dated back to 1740, though it had rarely been invoked before Louis Napoleon's days at the Elysée. His motives were not difficult to discern. He wanted to extend French influence in the Middle East and at the same time attract Catholic support at home. His manoeuvres, however, brought him up against opposition from Russia, since the Turks had also conceded rights to the Orthodox Christians in the Holy Places, and the Tsar was the defender of Orthodoxy. By the end of 1852 French pressure, which included a naval show of force in the Bosphorus, appeared to have obtained satisfaction from the Porte. There matters might have rested, but for the Tsar's refusal to accept a diplomatic defeat.

In 1853 a mission headed by the imperious Prince Menshikov was dispatched to Constantinople to demand the dismissal of the Turkish foreign minister responsible for ruling in favour of the French. He also insisted on confirmation of Russia's right to act as protector of all the Greek Orthodox subjects of the Sultan, terms which, if conceded, would have permitted Russia to interfere in Turkish affairs more or less at will. The British, ever suspicious of Russian expansionism and solicitous for the sea route to India, were no less alarmed by the Tsar's pretensions than the French, who on Napoleon III's orders sent a fleet to Salamis. The Turks, heartened by the prospect of Anglo-French backing, stood firm against Russian pressure. War between Russia and Turkey began to look increasingly likely.

Napoleon III had no desire to see the conflict escalate into a general war. His preference, as always, was for the dispute to be resolved round the conference table. Indeed, so far from being eager for war, the Emperor disturbed the British ambassador and his own foreign minister, Drouyn de Lhuys, by giving the impression of being ready to abandon the Turks to the Russians.[4] In June 1853, mainly to cultivate good relations with Britain, he did agree to send a French fleet to Baku Bay to be ready to reply to any sudden Russian strike against Constantinople. His real hopes were pinned on a negotiated settlement in talks between representatives of France, Britain, Austria and Prussia in Vienna. Largely on the basis of proposals put forward by Drouyn, a formula was worked out which was acceptable to Russia. It was the Turks who, egged on by the Russophobe British ambassador in Constantinople, Stratford de Redcliffe, rejected the Vienna note and declared war on Russia in October 1853. Napoleon III was dismayed, and hoped that a swift defeat at the hands of the Russians would make the Sultan more pliable. He did not bargain on the annihilation of the Turkish fleet at Sinope on 30 November.

The prospect of the imminent dissolution of the Turkish Empire alarmed all the powers, none more so than Britain, where anti-Russian sentiment was stirred up by a press campaign denouncing the 'massacre' of Sinope. Napoleon, acutely aware that neither the business community nor the peasants in France wanted a general war, persisted with his efforts to find a negotiated settlement. At the same time, he proposed that a joint Franco-British fleet should enter the Black Sea to thwart Russian, but not Turkish, naval movements. It was these manoeuvres which prompted Nicholas I to react negatively to the personal letter of 29 January 1854 which Napoleon sent to him in a last-ditch effort to salvage peace. If the Russians would withdraw their forces from the principalities of Moldavia and Wallachia, Napoleon promised that the British and the French would withdraw their fleets from the Black Sea. Whether or not the offer was a genuine one remains a moot point, since Napoleon published the text of his letter in the *Moniteur* before the Tsar had a chance to reply. In any event, Nicholas rejected the proposal and told Napoleon that, in the eventuality of a conflict, France would find Russia as ready in 1854 as it had been in 1812. Committed to seeing off the Russian threat and to each other, France and Britain accepted the logic of war and opened hostilities on 27 and 28 March 1854.

On 10 April 1854 the two powers concluded a formal alliance and turned their sights towards taking Sebastopol (though initially conflict centred on the Baltic). A joint attack on the Russian stronghold in the Crimea was repulsed in September and the allied forces embarked on a protracted siege which turned into a nightmare for the cold, poorly provisioned, disease-stricken and badly led troops. To take Sebastopol became Napoleon's obsession. In February 1855 he made up his mind to go to the Crimea in person to take command of operations – a decision which caused consternation among both his own entourage and the British. First, however, to reinforce the British alliance, he agreed to pay a state visit to the United Kingdom, where in April 1855 he and Eugénie made a highly favourable impression on Queen Victoria. On his return, he narrowly survived an assassination attempt at the hands of an Italian named Pianori, who had vowed to kill him for having betrayed the Roman Republic. The precariousness of the dynasty was plain, and, rather than leave the unreliable Prince Napoleon and his father King Jerome in charge at home (for the Empress was bent on coming with him), Napoleon reluctantly abandoned the idea of going to the Crimea. Besides, by this time (May 1855) there was serious talk of peace.

In fact, diplomatic activity had intensified rather than disappeared after the outbreak of war, as both parties sought to cultivate the support of other powers, and notably of Austria and Prussia. On 8 August 1854, the British, French and Austrian governments drew up a four-point agreement on terms which would allow a settlement, and in December 1854 French diplomacy secured Austria as an ally (though not a combatant) on the understanding that, if Russia accepted the four points as the basis for talks, the Vienna negotiations could be reopened. Although the British showed little enthusiasm for these exchanges, Drouyn worked hard to produce terms acceptable to Russia and compatible with French honour. Napoleon, however, did not want to know about peace until he had secured a famous military victory. He therefore repudiated his foreign minister's efforts and obliged him to resign. Securing the military participation of Sardinia in January 1855 brought him some satisfaction, but the coveted triumph of arms eluded him until Sebastopol finally fell on 8 September 1855.

Napoleon was now ready to conclude peace as rapidly as possible, not least because public opinion in France was weary of a war which had cost 100,000 French lives. He did threaten to turn the war into a revolutionary crusade to redraw the map of Europe, conjuring up visions of a resuscitated Poland, a new northern Italian state free of Austrian rule, the transfer of Moldavia and Wallachia to Austria and compensation for Turkey in the Crimea. However sincerely Napoleon might have been attached to such schemes, he knew that they had no chance of realisation without the cooperation of his British ally. It is likely, therefore, that he put them forward less as practical propositions than as a ploy to hasten the end of a war which was in danger of dragging on because of Palmerston's enthusiasm for humiliating Russia. Napoleon's schemes also frightened his new Foreign Minister, Walewski, a Russophile, who was only too anxious to press ahead, in conjunction with Austria, with peace feelers to the new and less intransigent Tsar Alexander II, who by January 1856 was ready to negotiate seriously.

Napoleon ensured that the peace congress was held in Paris. It opened on 25 February, presided by Walewski. It was the Emperor himself, however, as Lord Clarendon testified, who was the single most important influence on the peacemaking process. The final terms, signed on 30 March 1856, gave him practically all of what he wanted. The Black Sea was neutralised: Russia lost southern Bessarabia to Moldavia: Moldavia, Wallachia and Serbia were granted autonomy: the traffic on the Danube was to be regulated by an international commission: and the Turks were obliged to give assurances regarding the good treatment of their Christian subjects. France made no material gains, but its prestige, and that of its Emperor, stood high. Napoleon would have liked to see a formal repudiation of the Vienna settlement, but even without this it was readily apparent that the Crimean War and the Treaty of Paris had effected a diplomatic revolution in smashing the Waterloo coalition and reaffirming French pre-eminence among the powers. The Congress of Paris had not redrawn the map of Europe in conformity with Napoleonic ideas, but the Emperor could hope that it had cleared the way for promoting them in the future. In 1856, things seemed to be going his way, especially when the Empress produced an heir during the peace negotiations. From nowhere, he had arrived as the leading statesman in Europe in just eight years.

## THE LIBERATOR?

For Napoleon III the Congress of Paris was not an end but a beginning. Having covered himself in glory, he was keen to press forward with his plans for redrawing the map of Europe. Of course, he still needed allies, and, realising that defeat might have made Russia into a revisionist power, rather than, as hitherto, the strongest bastion of the status quo, he began to woo the Tsar. During the Congress itself he earned the gratitude of the Russian representative, Count Orlov, for the way in which he ensured that the settlement of the Bessarabian and Principalities issues were not as detrimental to Russian interests as British policy-makers could have wished. Afterwards, Morny was sent as ambassador to St Petersburg. Though well-received, he was made to understand that the price Russia would require for sanctioning any aggrandisement of France was the annulment of the Black Sea clauses of the Treaty of Paris – a price Napoleon III was not ready to pay, because it would have cost him the British alliance, to which he still attached maximum importance.

That alliance was tested by a number of crises which arose almost as soon as the Paris peace talks ended. The first arose over the matter of the Bessarabian frontier, when Palmerston protested about Russian attempts to subvert the spirit if not the letter of the provisions in the Treaty. Napoleon III seized the opportunity to exploit Anglo-Russian difficulties and, expressing sympathy for the Russian position, suggested a return to conference diplomacy to resolve the issue. In the end he personally was responsible for drawing up a boundary line that was satisfactory to both the British and the Russians. The position in the Danubian Provinces also gave rise to tensions. On account of Turkish interference in their elections, France and Russia, backed by Sardinia and Prussia, broke off diplomatic relations with the Sultan in August 1857. The problem was compounded by the support of Russia and Napoleon III (but not that of Walewski or the French Ambassador at Constantinople, Thouvenel) for a union of Moldavia and Wallachia and their independence from Turkey, whereas Britain and Austria preferred to see them remain separate and under Turkish suzerainty. Once again, it was Napoleon's skilful diplomatic manoeuvres which produced a solution in the direction he favoured, though not without leaving the British convinced that he had duped them. Another conference held in Paris, in March 1858, decided on the creation of the United Principalities of Moldavia and Wallachia, not yet the single state which Napoleon III and Romanian nationalists would have preferred, but twin states, largely autonomous and permanently allied, with a common legal system and army.

Napoleonic diplomacy also facilitated the resolution of the status of Neuchâtel, a territory disputed by the King of Prussia and the Swiss. In 1856 Frederick William of Prussia threatened force against the Swiss authories for refusing to release Prussian royalists apprehended in an abortive attempt to take over the castle on behalf of their king. As always, Napoleon was willing to propose a conference in Paris to settle the matter. In March 1857, he put forward a compromise solution by which the Swiss federal government, reluctantly and under French pressure, agreed to release their prisoners unconditionally, and a short time afterwards the Prussian king voluntarily renounced his claims to Neuchâtel.

In all these incidents, and others such as his support for Montenegro against the Turks in 1858, Napoleon III could be represented both as the champion of liberal and national causes and as a practitioner of a new style of congress diplomacy, which aimed at the resolution of conflicts without war. It makes more sense, however, to see them as occasions which the Emperor seized in order to give France the diplomatic initiative and to help prepare the way for the general reorganisation of the map of Europe that was his consuming ambition. Nor had force been ruled out in pursuit of this goal, as the case of Italy, perhaps the key test of all that the *politique des nationalités* implied, soon demonstrated.

Napoleon III's sympathy for the Italian cause was of long standing. In power, however, he had done little to promote it. Rather the reverse: Italian patriots were still indignant about his role in the crushing of the Roman Republic in 1849, while those who had hoped to see some prominence given to the affairs of Italy at the Congress of Paris were again disappointed, despite the participation of Piedmont-Sardinia in the Crimean War. Indeed, desperate Italian revolutionaries, as we have seen, made several attempts on Napoleon III's life, the most serious of which was the bomb attack of 14 January 1858 by Felice Orsini and his collaborators, which claimed the lives of eight bystanders outside the Opéra and wounded 152 others. The fact that the bombs had been made in London, and that the assassins had travelled on British passports, further strained relations not only with the Sardinians but also with the British. With anti-British sentiment running high in the country, Napoleon had no option but to protest to London as well as to Turin at the succour given to terrorists. In the aftermath of the Orsini attack, it seemed that the Italian cause had received yet another setback.

Paradoxically, it was Orsini's bombs which finally galvanised the Emperor into doing something for Italy. While awaiting trial, Orsini issued a dramatic appeal to Napoleon, urging him to become the liberator of Italy. Impressed, and doubtless already beginning to see the political possibilities that the Orsini affair offered, Napoleon gave permission for Orsini's letter, which had been delivered personally into his hands by his Corsican chief of police, Piétri, to be read out in court by counsel for the defence, the Republican lawyer, Jules Favre. Even more sensationally, he gave permission for it to be reproduced in *Le Moniteur* and other newspapers, which immediately brought protests from Austria. After Orsini and his co-defendants had been found guilty, Napoleon was even tempted to commute the death sentence (for the Empress and other society ladies had all been enchanted by the dignified conduct of the noble and handsome Orsini at his trial) but he was overruled by his ministers, who pointed out that to spare Orsini would be interpreted as a sign of weakness. The murderer went to his fate on 13 March, but Napoleon III wasted no time in moving decisively towards a pro-Italian and anti-Austrian foreign policy. The same month, through the channel of Dr Conneau, his personal physician, he indicated to Victor Emmanuel and his chief minister, Cavour, that France was ready to ally with Piedmont to expel Austria from northern Italy. Through his wife, he dropped hints to the subtle Piedmontese ambassador, Nigra, as to how he envisaged the reshaping of the Italian peninsula. Most important of all, he set up a secret meeting with Cavour at the spa of Plombières for 20 July 1858.

Cavour arrived incognito, travelling on a false passport, thus adding to the atmosphere of conspiracy. What was decided was nothing less than a plot to provoke a war with Austria. In a matter of hours, during which Napoleon took Cavour for a drive through the Vosges, the two men concocted a plan whereby France and Piedmont would become allies committed to the expulsion of Austria from northern Italy by force of arms. After the war, Piedmont would acquire Lombardy and Venetia, along with the duchies of Parma, Modena and Lucca and the Marches, to permit the establishment of a Sardinian Kingdom of Northern Italy. There would also be a new Kingdom of Central Italy, consisting of Tuscany and the Papal States in Umbria, and headed by the Duchess of Parma. The Pope would be the ruler of another state centred on Rome and its surrounding territory. The Kingdom of Naples would stay as it was, unless liberated by popular revolution. All four states would combine in a federation presided over by the Pope. France would be compensated with Savoy and possibly also Nice. The Emperor also proposed a dynastic alliance involving the marriage of Victor Emmanuel's daughter Princess Clotilde to his cousin Prince Napoleon. That Napoleon III was the prime mover in these schemes is clear from his insistence that the war be engineered in such a way as to make Austria rather than France seem the aggressor in the eyes of international opinion. His suggestion was that a suitable *casus belli* might be found from exploiting the situation in Modena, where Piedmontese agents should foment unrest with a view to provoking appeals for protection against Austria to Sardinia (and therefore France). The provisions regarding the Pope also reflected Napoleon's hopes of mitigating the antagonism sure to be expressed by French Catholics in the event of a war with Austria.[5]

Plombières was one of the key events of nineteenth-century European history. What passed between the two conspirators later became known through the publication of Cavour's correspondence. His account of the meeting to his sovereign remains, in the words of former Austrian ambassador Hübner, 'one of the most important historical documents and one best suited to throw light on the character and reign of Napoleon III'.[6] Here is the refutation of Napoleon's claim that the Empire meant peace. War was never ruled out as a policy option, as he had already demonstrated in the Crimea. Here, too, is the real meaning of the *politique des nationalités*: a pretext for the aggrandisement of France under cover of promoting a limited degree of nationalism. Italy was to be kept divided, not united. France would replace Austria as the dominant influence in northern Italy and reinforce its position as a Mediterranean power. Far from being a contribution to the principle of national self-determination, Plombières was an exercise in the diplomacy of *Realpolitik*. Napoleon was the true master of the art, with Cavour a mere amateur by comparison.[7] At Plombières he revealed a cynicism, a duplicity, an opportunism and a total absence of any moral sense which, as Hübner rightly said, made him the equal of any Italian Renaissance prince. In Cavour's letter, one recognises a sovereign who, in Hübner's words, was 'a dreamer, a gambler, a conspirator by taste and habit'. Any assessment of Napoleon III which overlooks Plombières (and it is an episode on which his admirers do not always care to dwell) must fail to capture his astonishing amorality and his bewildering contradictions. How was he to be the nephew of Napoleon and a defender of the peace? The brother of legitimist monarchs and a friend of revolution? The champion of nationalities and the guardian of treaties? The elected choice of the people and a military conspirator? He himself never resolved these tensions, for, in addition to lacking principles, he also lacked priorities. After Plombières, Cavour was under no illusion that Napoleon would necessarily keep his word. His track record of keeping promises was, after all, not good. Cavour may even have exaggerated the Emperor's commitment to the hazardous enterprise in order to encourage his own sovereign.

The details worked out at Plombières were, of course, kept secret, even from Napoleon III's ministers. But Cavour had been spotted, and word soon leaked out about their rendezvous, accompanied by not inaccurate forecasts in the Italian press of what it portended – namely, war with Austria the following year. Napoleon knew that he needed to proceed with the utmost caution. In early August, he began to express doubts to Nigra about the quasi-Mazzinian plan he had devised to provoke Austria, and Cavour was obliged to write to him to stiffen his resolve. Alarmed that the other powers might act to forestall France and Sardinia, Napoleon dispatched Prince Napoleon to Russia to discover the price of the Tsar's support, or at least neutrality. It was still the same. Negotiations eventually produced an agreement with Russia, signed on 3 March 1859, whereby the Tsar agreed to countenance the expulsion of Austria from northern Italy on condition that, in any congress which ensued from a war against Austria, France would support Russian requests for the revision of the Black Sea clauses of the Treaty of Paris – the very stipulation on which he had insisted with so much vigour in 1856. Napoleon's lack of principle had no limits.

In the meantime he attempted to allay the fears of Britain. On the occasion of the opening of the new docks at Cherbourg, he entertained Queen Victoria and Prince Albert and invited Palmerston and Clarendon to Compiègne, ostensibly to hunt but in reality to discuss the Italian situation. He also began to prepare French public opinion for war with Austria through a number of officially inspired newspaper articles.[8] The hapless Walewski, who was being cuckolded by the Emperor in addition to being bypassed in the making of foreign policy, issued placatory statements, but they carried little conviction.

One signal widely believed to be indicative of Napoleon's intentions was his remark to Hübner, the Austrian ambassador, on New Year's Day 1859, to the effect that Franco-Austrian relations were 'no longer so good as formerly'.[9] Made in the hearing of other ambassadors, the Emperor's words caused a sensation both abroad and at home, where the stock market plunged at the prospect of war. Napoleon protested that he had been misunderstood, and that what he wanted was a genuine improvement in relations with Austria. Yet all the while he remained in contact with Cavour, working out how best to proceed with their schemes and refining the arrangements made at Plombières. Cavour sent him the draft of Victor Emmanuel's speech from the throne, to be delivered on 10 January, and he altered it to make it sound more threatening. On 30 January 1859, he told Sardinia that France must definitely be rewarded with Nice as well as Savoy, and that Sardinia must underwrite the costs incurred by French troops on top of their own. More publicly, the marriage was announced of the Princess Clotilde and Plon-Plon. When the couple returned to Paris on 3 February, they were greeted at the station by an unnaturally silent crowd, which feared – rightly – that their union was linked to a military alliance, and presaged war.

Yet Napoleon may still have entertained notions that he could accomplish his designs by intimidation and war scares, without recourse to war itself. He had no moral scruples about unleashing war, but he could not be indifferent to the general feeling that war was undesirable. As he wrote to Prince Napoleon on 27 January, 'Public opinion in Europe is still rising against me, and even more against you: it is thought that we want war'.[10] At all costs he wanted to avoid the odium he would incur were France to appear the aggressor. On 4 February 1859, the *Moniteur* carried an article entitled '*L'Empéreur Napoléon III et l'Italie*', purporting to be written by a journalist, but in fact dictated by Napoleon III himself. It denounced Austrian rule in Italy, extolled Sardinia and revived the old Napoleonic plan for an Italian federation of states headed by the Pope. It suggested, however, that whereas 'The Emperor Napoleon I thought it right to conquer peoples in order to liberate them, Napoleon III wished to liberate them without conquering them'. Yet the use of force was not ruled out, for the article also contained a threat: 'We ardently hope that diplomacy may accomplish before a conflict what it will certainly do after a victory.' On 7 February, in his speech from the throne, his tone was more conciliatory, though ambiguity about his intentions remained. Having denounced the 'abnormal situation' in Italy, he went on to say, reassuringly, that it did not justify a war.[11] His hesitations continued into March, when, to the fury of Prince Napoleon and other *italianissimes* in his entourage, he agreed to go along with Russian proposals to call a congress to settle the Italian problem. Explaining his policy to Walewski in a letter of 25 March, he told his minister that his goal was above all to isolate Austria at the congress. As for Sardinia:

here is what I intend to tell Cavour.

The question of Italy has been badly presented; the congress will replace it on a good footing. Today I cannot make war without great danger. Wait for the solution of the questions brought forward at the congress and help me to find and advance them.

If, as I hope, the congress takes a decision contrary to Austria, the war will come in good circumstances. If, on the contrary, Austria yields on all points, it will be necessary to console ourselves and to postpone the game until another day.[12]

Napoleon was willing to contemplate the possibility that somehow he might manage to have his way in Italy without having to fight. It should be noticed, however, that such an outcome was to be regarded as second best, and a matter for regret. Ideally, France and Sardinia would have their war, once the time was right. After all, for the maverick Emperor, it was only a 'game'.

The congress proposal appealed to French public opinion. Had the Austrians shown any flexibility, there is no certainty that Napoleon would have gone to war in order to keep his promises to Cavour. But the Austrians proved to be intransigent, rejecting the possibility of change in Italy, and demanding instead the disarmament of Sardinia. On 23 April they issued an ultimatum. The Sardinians chose to fight rather than back down before an Austrian threat and, as Austria appeared to have sabotaged the search for a negotiated settlement, the other powers maintained their neutrality when France joined the war alongside its Sardinian ally. After Austria had invaded Sardinian territory, Napoleon III issued a proclamation stating French objections to Austrian dominance all the way up to the French Alps, and calling for Italy to be freed to the Adriatic. French war aims were not conquest but 'to restore Italy to the Italians'. Napoleon went to war speaking the language of a liberator, though he soon proved to be a not disinterested one.

Having been prevented from taking command in the Crimea, the Emperor was determined to put himself at the head of his troops in Italy. Leaving Eugénie as regent, he set off from Paris on 10 May, to the ringing cheers of the fervently nationalist workers and radicals in the popular quarters of the capital. The combined Franco-Piedmontese force of 270,000 men was placed under his command. The Emperor was no military genius (though, if General Fleury can be believed, he was a more talented military commander than historians often allege)[13] but he did not have to be, faced with Austrian incompetence. Two victories followed in quick succession at the bloody battles of Magenta (4 June) and Solferino (24 June).

Then, abruptly, and to the dismay of Cavour, he called a halt to the fighting. His motives, as always, are difficult to fathom, but the most likely explanation is that he was afraid of Prussian intervention on the Austrian side, obliging him to fight on two fronts. He also knew that it would not be easy to inflict a further defeat on the Austrians: some of the limitations of his own army had been revealed in the fighting and, with the Austrian troops now entrenched in their great defensive fortresses of the Quadrilateral, victory might be a long way off. At the same time, French public opinion, gratified by his initial successes, was becoming restive at the prospect of a long war, with conservatives and clericals particularly alarmed by the outbreak of revolution in Central Italy on 11 June, which threatened the position of the Pope.

On 6 July Napoleon therefore proposed a truce, and two days later, in a meeting at Villafranca with the youthful Francis Joseph, who had personally commanded the Austrian troops at Solferino, he concluded an armistice, the terms of which were later incorporated into the Treaty of Zurich of 10 November 1859. Austria agreed to cede Lombardy to Piedmont (via France), except for the fortresses of the Quadrilateral. An Italian Confederation was to be established under the Pope. Austria would retain Venetia, but agree to internal reforms. The Duchies would continue to be ruled by Habsburg princes, but they would no longer be able to call upon foreign assistance to maintain their position by force in defiance of their subjects' wishes. The Papal States, including the Romagna, would continue to be subject to the temporal rule of the Pope.

For Napoleon III, Villafranca was an escape route from a potentially difficult situation. For Victor Emmanuel and Cavour it was a betrayal. In any case, it was rapidly overtaken by events. An agreement between Napoleon III and Francis Joseph did not deter Italian nationalists from carrying on their revolutions. Encouraged by Piedmontese agents, in August and September 1859 the new governments in Tuscany, Parma, Modena and the Romagna consulted their electorates on the issue of whether or not to unite with Sardinia. The vote was overwhelmingly in favour of union, and for an end to the rule of the princes (including the Pope in the Romagna). Not only Villafranca, but also Napoleon's schemes for a Central Italian state, now lay in ruins, for, to the chagrin of Francis Joseph, the Emperor refused to deploy French troops to restore the princes to their thrones. The Pope expressed his outrage at the depredation of papal territory in the Romagna, and Catholic opinion in France sympathised with him. Confronted with such different interests and pressures, Napoleon III fell back on his favourite idea of a European congress.

His plan was that the eight powers which had signed the Treaty of Vienna should reconvene in Paris, along with representatives of the three principal Italian states. The date of the congress was fixed for 19 January 1860. In order to prepare public opinion for his latest thoughts on the affairs of Italy, on 22 December 1859 Napoleon elected to publish an anonymous brochure entitled '*Le Pape et le Congrès*', which had been prepared by his ghost-writer, La Gueronnière, directly under his own supervision. Its contents were sensational, for the pamphlet argued the case for a reduction of the Pope's temporal power to embrace only Rome. Pius IX immediately issued his own strong condemnation of the plan in an encyclical of 19 January 1860.

Walewski, protesting that the brochure had been issued without his knowledge, let alone approval, resigned the Quai d'Orsay, to be replaced by the pro-Italian Thouvenel, recalled from the embassy at Constantinople. Clerical opinion at home was incensed, and the government was obliged to respond to their attacks with repression. *L'Univers*, the newspaper of the intransigent ultramontane journalist, Louis Veuillot, was banned, as was *La Bretagne*, another Catholic organ, for having published a letter from three deputies from Brittany denouncing the Piedmontese takeover of the Romagna. Clerics were more difficult to silence, however, and a number of bishops subverted the government's ban on the papal encyclical by having their clergy read it out at Mass. The Italian question had now created a serious breach between the Empire and the Church, hitherto one of its staunchest supporters. On the other hand, liberals and anticlericals were delighted as well as surprised by the new developments, while public opinion as a whole, as refracted through the reports of the *procureurs généraux* and the prefects, appears to have accepted that the Pope should resign himself to the loss of the Romagna. '*Le Pape et le Congrès*' also helped Napoleon III's image abroad, at least in Britain and Sardinia, but whether by accident or design, it sabotaged the congress itself, since neither the Papacy nor Austria was prepared to negotiate over the Romagna, and Britain saw no point in attending a conference that was unable to produce any positive results.

The failure of the congress idea left Napoleon III free to pursue French interests more overtly. Well aware that French opinion wanted to see some tangible gain for France as a result of the liberation of Lombardy, he began to manoeuvre for the cession of Nice and Savoy, on the grounds that, even if Italy had not been freed to the Adriatic, as promised, Piedmont-Sardinia had been able to expand to the south. Cavour reluctantly agreed to the deal in the Treaty of Turin, signed on 24 March 1860, which made it subject to a favourable vote by plebiscite from the populations in the territories concerned. After an overwhelming majority voted for annexation, Savoy and Nice were officially transferred to France on 14 June 1860. The new acquisition caused general delight in France and boosted the Emperor's popularity, nowhere more than in the south-east of the country, where he made a triumphal tour in August 1860. Foreign reactions were cooler, if not hostile. The British were more than ever convinced of Napoleon's duplicity and untrustworthiness, having rightly identified a desire for French aggrandisement behind all his lofty assertions of the principle of nationality.

At this juncture, Napoleon III was ready to rid himself of the affairs of Italy. That turned out to be more difficult than he had anticipated. The problem was Rome: how could he withdraw without abandoning the Pope to the Revolution, which would damage French prestige and infuriate French Catholics? The creation of an international army of Catholic volunteers under General Lamoricière seemed to give him his opportunity. In May 1860 he concluded an agreement with the Papacy which provided for an evacuation of French forces within three months. Yet his inability to control the destiny of Italy was soon to be cruelly exposed once more, for on 5 May, the very day of the Franco-Papal convention, Garibaldi, a patriot whose nationalism was further fuelled by the loss to France of his native Nice, set sail from Genoa for Sicily with his 1,000 red-shirts to begin the liberation of southern Italy from oppressive Bourbon rule, and to unite the whole peninsula.

Napoleon was placed in an extremely awkward situation. Conservative opinion in France, expressed in the clerical and Legitimist press, raised an outcry against Garibaldi. Veuillot's new paper *Le Monde* darkly prophesied the downfall of the papal monarchy. By contrast, not only did radical opinion enthusiastically support him (*L'Opinion Nationale*, the mouthpiece of Prince Napoleon, opened a subscription fund for the expedition) but even Orleanist organs like the *Revue des Deux Mondes* and the *Journal des Débats* gave guarded signs of approval. Napoleon also had to wrestle with the dilemma that a united Italy, while not an objective in line with traditional notions of French interests, embodied for him the idea of progress. It was certainly unthinkable that a French army should prop up a reactionary Bourbon regime against the aspirations of the southern Italian people. Not for the first time, Napoleon was perplexed by Italian events and, in the absence of any concerted move on the part of the great powers, played for time.

His first thought was to try to persuade the British to send a joint task force to prevent Garibaldi from being able to cross over to the Italian mainland. When the British rejected the proposal, he and Thouvenel opted for non-intervention as the only sensible policy. Frustrated by the mistrust about his ultimate ambitions which were widespread in Britain, he sought to allay suspicions by taking the extraordinary step of writing an open letter to Persigny, now his ambassador in London. Without consulting his foreign minister, he announced, via the British and French press on 1–2 August 1860, that the single objective of French foreign policy was 'to inaugurate a new era of peace and to live on the best terms with my neighbours, especially with Britain'. The British were mistaken to mistrust him for building up the French navy, which, he claimed, was in reality smaller than at the time of the July Monarchy. Such conquests as he had to make were not abroad but in France, developing the country's internal resources. Thus France and Britain should work hard to achieve genuine mutual understanding and to banish jealousies and rivalries. As far as Italy was concerned, he declared that it should be 'pacified no matter how, provided I can get out of Rome without compromising the safety of the Pope and that there is no foreign intervention'.[14] This astonishingly frank document expresses Napoleon's experience of the frustrations of power, rather than any ability to shape events in line with his wishes. They were certainly not the words of a liberator, and still less of an arbiter.

Such straight talking appalled his foreign minister, and disturbed nationalist sentiment at home by its over-deferential attitude to Britain. British policy-makers, cynical as ever, were impervious to his pleas, and doubted whether the letter could be taken at face value. In Italy, Cavour calculated that Napoleon would not act alone to thwart Garibaldi's enterprise, and he turned his mind to how best to exploit the turn of events in the south to the benefit of the House of Savoy. His first thought was to provoke a revolution in Naples, which would allow the King to turn to Victor Emmanuel for protection, but the stratagem misfired. As Garibaldi advanced up the peninsula, he devised a different plan: Victor Emmanuel and the Piedmontese army would themselves occupy the Papal States and the Marches, and then receive southern Italy from Garibaldi. The danger was that Napoleon might present himself as the champion of the Pope, but through emissaries sent to him while he toured his newly acquired territories of Nice and Savoy at the end of August, Cavour learned that the French Emperor would persist with his policy of non-intervention. In this way, Napoleon effectively gave his blessing to a united Italy – with more conviction, it would seem, than Thouvenel believed was warranted by the situation. When other options had been ruled out, he could return to playing the congenial role of liberator.

Garibaldi entered Naples on 7 September. The next day Cavour sent an ultimatum to the Pope, threatening an invasion of the Marches and Umbria if foreign troops were not removed from the papal army. When the demand was rejected, on 10 September Sardinia invaded papal territory. At the time, Napoleon III was away from Paris in the south of France, preparing for a trip to Algeria. Thouvenel telegraphed the Emperor to warn him that, if he did not publicly reprove the actions of Sardinia, he would be held accountable for them both abroad and at home. So Napoleon went through the motions of protesting against the Sardinian invasion, withdrawing his ambassador from Turin and reinforcing the French garrison at Rome, but informing his bemused foreign minister that he meant to threaten, not to act. Cavour had no difficulty in appreciating the Emperor's position, and knew that he would accept tacitly what he disavowed publicly.

Sardinian troops defeated the papal forces at Castelfidardo and Ancona to make themselves masters of the two papal provinces. They then advanced on Naples, entering in triumph on 7 November, with Victor Emmanuel accompanied by Garibaldi, who in prior negotiations had agreed to hand over his irregular army to the Piedmontese sovereign. Bourbon forces resisted at the port of Gaeta for another three and a half months, during which time Napoleon III sent a French fleet in token support. It did not engage in battle with the Piedmontese, nor did the latter open fire, and it was withdrawn in January 1861. Gaeta fell in mid-February. Victor Emmanuel was proclaimed king of the whole of Italy, except for Venetia and a much reduced Papal State. A new united Italy had come into being, partly because of the policies of Napoleon III, but also, in larger part, in spite of them.

## THE FRUSTRATIONS OF POWER

After 1860 Napoleon continued to be more at the mercy of events than in control of them. The affairs of Italy still plagued him. Rome was now the central problem: was it to remain under the Pope or should it become, as the Italian patriots demanded, the capital of their new state? Garibaldi's Sicilian expedition and, still more, the defeat of the papal army at Castelfidardo, prevented Napoleon III from withdrawing his troops as planned. Negotiations with cavour over the sorts of guarantees which he could provide for the Papacy to permit the French to leave had produced no agreement when the Piedmontese statesman died suddenly in June 1861. A combination of papal intransigence and the refusal of the other powers to entertain his projects for a European congress on the Roman question left him thwarted.

The situation deteriorated after July 1862, when Garibaldi tried to resolve the issue by a march on Rome with another band of irregular troops, and had to be stopped by the Italian army at Aspromonte. The Italian government, embarrassed at having to take up arms against a national hero, called for an immediate French withdrawal from Rome, an ultimatum which violated Napoleon's conception of French honour. Thouvenel persisted with his efforts to find a compromise, but the Emperor, ever sensitive to public opinion, and anxious not to appear wholly in the camp of the *italianissimes* as the legislative elections of 1863 approached, preferred to part with his foreign minister and recall the pro-Austrian Drouyn, a figure altogether more reassuring to conservatives. From the reports of his *procureurs généraux*, Napoleon knew that the great mass of the French people was indifferent to the Roman question, and he reckoned that for the time being he had more to gain by cultivating the support of the Church and conservatives than by posing as the champion of Italian nationalism.[15] The election results confirmed his belief that, provided he did not appear to abandon the Pope, he could continue to pursue negotiations for withdrawal with the Italian government. In April 1864, talks restarted and, at the end of five months, they produced the Convention of 15 September 1864, which envisaged a French departure from Rome within two years, while Italy undertook to guarantee the existing territories of the Pope. It looked like a settlement, but, as Napoleon was shortly to discover, the Roman question refused to go away.

The affairs of Poland likewise underlined the limitations on his power in the international arena. The Polish struggle to re-establish an independent state was one which had long engaged the Emperor's sympathies. As a young man, he had been tempted to join the insurrection of 1831, while during the Crimean War, he had at one stage threatened to unleash a 'revolutionary' crusade to free the Poles from Russian oppression. At the Paris peace talks of 1856 he had raised the possibility that at least the 'Congress' Kingdom of Poland, abolished by Russia in the aftermath of the 1831 rising, might be revived. When the Poles rose in revolt against the Tsar once again in January 1863, however, Napoleon was placed in an embarrassing position, since he had been assiduously cultivating good relations with Russia. Yet the plight of Poland was one of the very few issues capable of generating sympathy among Frenchmen of all ideological persuasions – Catholics, republicans and liberals. Public opinion expected France to 'do something' for Poland. But what? In the past Napoleon had criticised Louis Philippe for his failure to act, but in power he himself resisted the promptings of such as his cousin Prince Jerome, who in a memorandum of February 1863 called upon him to take up arms on behalf of the Poles and then proceed to a complete redrawing of the map of Europe.[16] Plon-Plon's 'dream', as Napoleon III called it, was also his own, but it was not one he could indulge without alienating the other powers. He had to proceed with the utmost caution, knowing full well that most of those Frenchmen who expressed sympathy for Poland did not want to see France become embroiled in war as a result.

To act alone against Russia was unthinkable. In any case, if possible, he wanted to preserve the friendship of the Tsar. Napoleon and Drouyn therefore tried initially to identify Prussia rather than Russia as the villain of the piece for having concluded with Russia, on 8 February, the Alvensleben Convention, by which Bismarck promised Prussian assistance to help put down the Polish rebels. On 21 February, Drouyn invited Britain and Austria to join with France in protesting to Berlin against the Alvensleben Convention, but their response was cool. Sympathy for the Poles was widespread in Britain, but the government had no intention of becoming involved in their affairs. Nor were British policy-makers unhappy to see France and Russia divided over Poland. The Austrians, worried that Polish nationalism might spread to their own territory of Galicia, had every reason to be negative, though they went out of their way to signal that they wished to have good relations with the two western powers.

The idea of isolating Prussia was more Drouyn's than Napoleon's. The Emperor soon showed signs that, after all, the Polish crisis might be an opportunity to effect the kind of sweeping changes which accorded with 'Napoleonic ideas' and had been suggested in Prince Napoleon's memorandum. The way forward seemed to be to associate Austria with his schemes, and to link the Italian problem with the Polish problem. Between late February and the end of March 1863, Napoleon pushed hard to secure an Austrian alliance. Eugénie, an intimate friend of the Austrian ambassador, Metternich, and his wife, lent her enthusiastic support, on one occasion treating the envoy to her own redrawing of the map of Europe.[17]

Less dramatically, but with similar wide-ranging implications for the European order, Napoleon gave Metternich to understand that he wished to see Austria give up Galicia, and also Venetia, in return for which Austria would be compensated in the east and in Germany. Under the entreaties of the imperial couple, Metternich decided to recommend the alliance to his masters in Vienna. They, however, rejected it. Rechberg wrote officially to Drouyn to say that, because his country was engaged in a demanding programme of internal reform, it was unable to participate in the kind of active policy, potentially involving long and costly wars, which a French alliance might entail. His more substantial objections were set out in secret instructions to Metternich, where the value which Austria attached to both Galicia and Venetia was made plain, along with wider fears about making any concessions to the principle of nationalities.[18] The proposed compensations were inadequate for the loss of two key provinces of the Empire.

While Napoleon pursued his unsuccessful quest for an Austrian alliance, the British were preparing proposals of their own with regard to the Polish question, namely, that the signatories of the Vienna Treaty should deliver a collective note to St Petersburg asking for restoration of the arrangements of 1815. Napoleon had little choice but to go along with the *démarche*, though the Austrians demurred, with the result that what finally happened was a simultaneous, but separate, set of protests presented by the British, French and Austrian ambassadors at St Petersburg on 17 April. Napoleon's own preference, however, remained to use the Polish crisis as a starting point for more far-reaching changes which could only be accomplished by his favourite device of a European congress. As his minister Billault told the Legislative Body on 20 March, 'the Polish question is European and it is with the aid of Europe that the imperial government intends to resolve it'.[19] In May–June, Napoleon tried to convoke a conference which would not confine itself to the issue of Poland. The suspicions of the other powers were aroused, but in any case, in July, the Russians, having bought time by playing along with the idea, finally rejected a congress as an intrusion into their domestic affairs.

Still the Emperor persisted with one of his favourite ploys. In early November 1863, without consulting Drouyn, he sent out invitations to all European rulers (not just the sovereigns of the great powers) to attend a congress in Paris. Outlining his motives for this bold step to the French legislature on 5 November, he explained that the Polish question offered an opportunity to reorganise Europe along new lines, and to break definitively with the settlement of 1815, which had already effectively ceased to exist. A congress could 'lay the foundations of a general pacification'. Two choices were available: 'One leads to progress by way of reconciliation and peace; the other, sooner or later, will take us fatalistically to war, as the consequence of an obstinate determination to maintain a crumbling past.'[20] Neither Prussia nor Russia rejected Napoleon's scheme out of hand, but Austria made plain its unwillingness to allow the transfer of Galicia or Venetia to be part of any agenda, while the British firmly vetoed a congress.

The Emperor took rejection of his plans badly. Cowley claimed never to have seen him 'so morose or out of spirits'.[21] The Russians completed their work of repression in Poland, and, yet another time, Napoleon's inability to implement his ideas by means of diplomacy was cruelly exposed. Indeed, his international standing was seriously weakened, for his representations on behalf of Poland had cost him the good will of Russia, while the wounding manner of the British rejection of his congress proposal was a signal that the Anglo-French alliance, already severely strained, was now at an end. The real beneficiary of the Polish crisis was Prussia, to whom the Russians began to look as a more solid and reliable ally than France. Resentful and withdrawn after the Polish episode, Napoleon failed to appreciate the dangers which Prussia had already begun to pose to French security. Between 1861 and 1862 the size of the Prussian army had been almost doubled, and, with Bismarck as Minister-President, the state was now committed to a policy of 'blood and iron'.

The new military machine did not have long to wait to be put to the test. When the new Danish king, Christian IX, was imprudent enough to try to enforce his country's claims to the duchies of Schleswig and Holstein at the expense of those of the German Confederation, Prussia, backed by Austria, declared war on 1 February 1864. Sentiment in France was strongly pro-Danish, all the more so as the war went on, but as in the case of Poland there was no demand in favour of French intervention. Sore at the treatment which his own congress proposals had received, Napoleon III affected a disinterested attitude to the whole affair, opposing British attempts to work out a negotiated settlement before the outbreak of hostilities, and proposing instead a referendum among the peoples of the duchies. The war, briefly interrupted by unsuccessful peace talks in London, ended with the defeat of the Danes. In August 1864, they were compelled to hand over Schleswig and Holstein to Prussia and Austria. Napoleon may have been right to stay out of the conflict, as no vital French interests were involved, and there was always the hope that he might win Prussian friendship in the future, but, even had he wanted to, he would have been unable to play the role of arbiter of Europe in the Danish conflict. His neutrality may have been calculated, but, given his refusal to act in concert with Britain, it was also necessary. Napoleon III was painfully aware that he alone could not control Europe's destiny.

. . .

## NOTES AND REFERENCES

1. Cf. Mosse W E 1958 *The European Powers and the German Question 1848–1871: with Special Reference to England and Russia.* Cambridge University Press. Jerrold B 1882 *The Life of Napoleon III.* Longman, vol 4, p. 157 describes the Emperor as 'the arbiter of the destinies of Europe'

2. Echard W E 1983 *Napoleon III and the Concert of Europe.* Louisiana State University Press

3. Kinglake A W 1863–80 *The Invasion of the Crimea: Its Origin and an Account of Its Progress down to the Death of Lord Raglan,* 6 vols, Blackwood

4. Echard 1983, p. 31

5. Cavour Count C B 1926–29 *Il carteggio Cavour – Nigra dal 1858 al 1861* Edited by the governmental Commissione Reale Editrice dei Carteggi Cavouriani, 4 vols, Bologna, vol 1, pp. 103–10. English translation given in Mack Smith D 1968 *The Making of Italy.* Harper & Row, pp. 238–47

6. Hübner J A von 1904 *Neuf ans de souvenirs d'un ambassadeur d'Autriche à Paris sous le Second Empire 1851–1859,* p. 220

7. Some historians of Italy take the view that Cavour out-witted Napoleon at Plombières; cf. Hearder H 1983 *Italy in the Age of the Risorgimento 1790–1870.* Longman. Each man was of course making use of the other for his own purposes, but Napoleon was obviously the dominant partner

8. Isser N 1974 *The Second Empire and the Press: a Study of Government-inspired Brochures on French Foreign Policy in Their Propaganda Milieu.* Martinus Nijhoff

9. Hübner 1904

10. Hauterive E de 1925 *Napoléon III et le Prince Napoléon (Correspondance inédite)*

11. Eddleston *Napoleon III: Speeches from the Throne.* R I Severs, p. 169

12. Quoted by Echard 1983, p. 98

13. *Souvenirs du Général Comte Fleury 1837–1867,* 2 vols, 3rd edn, 1897–98

14. Quoted by Corley T A B 1961 *Democratic Despot: a Life of Napoleon III.* Barrie & Rockliff, p. 229

15. Case L 1954 *French Opinion on War and Diplomacy during the Second Empire.* University of Pennsylvania Press, p. 159

16. Echard 1983, p. 159

17. Barker N N 1968 *Distaff Diplomacy: the Empress Eugenie and the Foreign Policy of the Second Empire*, University of Texas Press, discusses Eugénie's (minimal) influence on French foreign policy
18. Hallberg C W 1955 *Franz Joseph and Napoleon III 1852–1864: a Study of Austro-French Relations*. Octagon Books
19. Echard 1983, p. 154
20. Ibid., p. 196
21. Ibid., p. 203

# Chapter 7

# POWER WITHOUT GLORY
## (1864–70)

In the aftermath of the Danish war, French policy seemed to lack direction. Napoleon badly wanted to regain the diplomatic initiative, but he discovered that he was less than ever able to shape events to his will. In part, he was the victim of bad luck: the cards refused to fall in his favour, and he had to play against greater odds. But in part, too, he was let down by his own judgement. The gambler lost his winning touch, and entered on a losing streak. He remained an opportunist, but he no longer always knew how to take his chances.

. . .

## SADOWA

The affairs of Italy, which had afforded Napoleon some tangible benefits in 1859–60, seemed to offer most scope for further gains. Venetia remained unredeemed, despite his pledge to Cavour to free Italy 'to the Adriatic'. He determined to force a solution. The right opportunity seemed to hand over the quarrel which had brewed up between Austria and Prussia.

Ostensibly, the Austrians and the Prussians were at odds over how to divide the spoils of their recent war against Denmark. In 1865 they almost went to war themselves, until Bismarck succeeded in patching up an agreement in the Gastein Convention, which gave the two powers joint sovereignty over the annexed duchies of Schleswig and Holstein. Few people, Napoleon III included, had any faith that this compromise would provide the basis of a durable settlement, since behind the Schleswig-Holstein issue there lurked the larger question of Prussian and Austrian rivalry for the leadership of Germany. The new Prussian Minister-President was bent on a showdown, and convinced that war was essential to establish Prussian dominance. How France would react in the event of an Austro-Prussian war was crucial to his calculations, and his ambitions for Prussia therefore presented Napoleon III with a rare opportunity to appear in the role of power-broker.

Bismarck took potential French opposition seriously. Though he later claimed in his memoirs to have taken the measure of Napoleon III early, reckoning him 'not so shrewd as the world thinks him', Bismarck did not make the mistake of underestimating his opponent.[1] The Prussian statesman was by nature inclined to slight his fellow men and to vaunt his own superiority, but Napoleon III clearly impressed him by providing the model of a ruler who managed to combine the principle of authority with elements of democracy, while succeeding at the same time in pursuing an ambitious and revisionist foreign policy. In the run-up to the Austro-Prussian War, Bismarck went to considerable pains to divine the French Emperor's intentions, and to win him over to his schemes for the reorganisation of northern Germany.

In October 1864, he joined Napoleon at Biarritz, and hinted that France might hope to obtain Belgium or Luxembourg as the price for backing Prussia. Napoleon was non-committal, noting only Bismarck's generosity 'in giving away what does not belong to him'.[2] In October and early November 1865, Bismarck returned to Biarritz by way of Paris and held a series of conversations (nine in all) with Napoleon III, Drouyn, Rouher and the Italian ambassador, Nigra. There is no record of Napoleon III's version of these conversations, but much of what passed between him and the Prussian Minister-President can be deduced from Bismarck's and Nigra's accounts. Bismarck wanted both to reassure France about the Gastein Convention and to persuade Napoleon to endorse his plans for an enlarged North German Confederation under Prussian leadership. Assuming that French compliance could not be obtained for nothing, he again floated the idea of 'compensation' in Belgium, and hinted at Prussian willingness to see Venetia incorporated into the new Italian state. Once more the French Emperor gave little away, though to Bismarck's relief he did not make any 'unwelcome demands' (meaning the Rhineland). He did, however, raise the Eastern question, and Prussia's relationship with Russia, which obliged Bismarck to explain that good relations between Prussia and Russia had to be maintained because of their long common frontier, and their mutual interest in Poland. Despite Nigra's assurances, Bismarck could not be certain that Napoleon would countenance an Italo-Prussian alliance. The most hopeful aspect of the interviews from Bismarck's point of view was that he detected in Napoleon a deep-seated antipathy to Austria, which encouraged him to believe that he would never ally with the Habsburgs. He could not be sure, but he sensed that, in the event of war with Austria, there was a strong possibility that France would maintain a benevolent neutrality.[3]

Did Napoleon III blunder at Biarritz? Many historians have thought so. One recent account describes the Biarritz conversations as 'the first step on the slope leading to Sedan and the fall of the Second Empire'.[4] This would appear to be a good example of the dangers of reading history backwards. Biarritz was a meeting of equals. Bismarck did not underrate Napoleon, but neither did he overestimate him. He went to Biarritz to weigh up the situation, not as a suppliant, and his grounds for satisfaction were considerable. For one thing, he gathered that the French Emperor was not in principle opposed to the creation of a Prussian-dominated German state, partly out of sympathy with the 'nationality' idea (and here it is important to recall that in the 1860s Prussia also enjoyed a reputation for being 'liberal' and 'progressive'), partly because of the blow it would inflict upon Austria and the remnants of the treaties of 1815, and partly because of what it might bring France by way of reward.

By 1865, Napoleon was also having to contend with a variety of domestic problems, notably the revival of political opposition in the country and in the Legislative Body, where Thiers and his faction constituted a strong lobby against any moves to involve France in the quarrel between Prussia and Austria. Most important of all, Bismarck could not be unaware of the dispersal of French armed forces – in Mexico, in Algeria, in Indo-China as well as the garrison in Rome, together with the prospect of further reductions in line with the retrenchment measures of Finance Minister Fould. All of these factors were constraints on Napoleon's freedom of action, quite apart from the problems of ill-health which, as we have already seen, had begun to surface at this time, and constituted a source of worry, even if they had little impact on his policy. In any case, with or without Napoleon, Bismarck was determined to press ahead with his plans for a remodelled Germany – though, if need be, he left Napoleon in no doubt that he would seek a reconciliation with Austria, and once again conjure up against France the 'Holy Alliance' of Prussia, Russia and Austria.

In the circumstances, Napoleon had every reason to proceed with caution and to opt to wait on events. His 'inactivity' at Biarritz was more apparent than real, allowing him maximum flexibility of response. The only alternative would have been to show outright opposition to Bismarck's schemes and to seek the Austrian alliance so ardently championed by the Empress and Drouyn. As he knew from the abortive alliance negotiations of 1863, the price of such an alliance would have been the repudiation of a 'Napoleonic' foreign policy and a commitment to the status quo. In his own eyes, Napoleon stood for movement, or he stood for nothing. Prussia, by contrast with Austria, was a force for change, and that is why he was ready to acquiesce in its aggrandisement. Prussia, too, could be the instrument which, through French good offices, could secure Venetia for Italy, with happy consequences for French–Italian relations and the reinforcement of French power in the Mediterranean. Moreover, in the event of a war between Austria and Prussia, Napoleon was not alone in believing that it would be protracted, leaving him free to step in as arbiter, free at last to proceed to the grand redrawing of the European map which he dreamed of.[5] The Emperor's decision to reserve his position made a lot of sense. Neither at Biarritz nor in the immediate aftermath of the talks did Napoleon show any signs of diminishing diplomatic skills, let alone any feebleness of will which presaged the end of his Empire.

On the contrary, in the first half of 1866 he appeared to have recaptured the diplomatic initiative. As tension mounted between Prussia and Austria, Napoleon spared no effort in his determination to secure Venetia for Italy. In February, he favoured a deal whereby the Austrians would be compensated with the Principalities if they ceded Venetia to the Italians (the 'nationality principle', it seems, was expendable in the case of the Romanians). At the same time, to step up the pressure on the Austrians, he encouraged the Italian government to incite Prussia to make war on them and to prepare for war itself. (So much for the pacifism and commitment to 'congress diplomacy' sometimes said to be the chief characteristics of his policy.) The Italian situation was still at the forefront of his mind when a conference to discuss the Romanian situation convened in Paris on 10 March 1866 (the crisis having been precipitated by the overthrow of Prince Couza, the ruler of the two Principalities). Drouyn was instructed to insist that, even if the other powers came up with an acceptable solution, the Emperor would abide by his position – which was the proposed exchange of Venetia for the Principalities. This suggestion antagonised the Russians as much as the Austrians: the Tsar deemed it 'unacceptable – even to the point of war'. The British were also unenthusiastic. Bowing to the inevitable, Napoleon allowed the conference to settle the affairs of Moldavia and Wallachia, and expressed his support for the candidature of Charles of Hohenzollern for the Romanian throne. But he still meant to find a way to have Venetia transferred to Italy.

That brought him back to the German question, where he now courted both German powers with the aim of redeeming Venetia no matter how their own quarrel turned out. By March, he knew that there was no possibility of obtaining Prussian agreement to any transfer of the Rhineland to France in return for a French alliance. While affirming his pro-Prussian sentiments to Ambassador Goltz, he therefore kept lines open to Austria, discussing neutrality and agreeing to a sizeable loan, as well as signing a commercial treaty between the two countries. His attitude to the negotiations between Italy and Prussia in March–April 1866 was fraught with ambiguity. Nigra reported that he favoured an alliance, but in Berlin French Ambassador Benedetti advised the Italians against signing, and described Bismarck as 'un diplomate maniaque'[6] (a description which could not unjustly be applied to Napoleon himself). The likeliest explanation for Napoleon's tortuous diplomacy was that he was hoping to bring sufficient pressure to bear on Austria to make Vienna cede Venetia without a war. By May, he was talking yet again about the need for a European congress, though after his rebuff in 1863 he was loath to take the initiative himself. Italy took up the idea for him, and the British and the Russians also agreed to exploratory talks with Drouyn on 15 May, which went well enough for France, Britain and Russia to invite Prussia, Austria and Italy to attend a congress in Paris. Prussia grudgingly accepted. On 31 May Austria replied that it would attend only if it were guaranteed in advance that no territorial changes would be discussed. It was a veto, and a trial of strength between Austria and Prussia became inevitable.

Napoleon knew that French public opinion wanted France to

keep clear of a German conflict. On 6 May 1866 he had made a public speech at Auxerre to answer Thiers and other parliamentary critics who were urging him to make himself the champion of the borders imposed on Germany in 1815. Proclaiming his detestation of the Vienna treaties, the Emperor hinted strongly that a war in Central Europe which would reverse them was something that both he and the French people desired. But the surveys of public opinion conducted by the *procureurs généraux* revealed that most people favoured peace at virtually any price.[7] Ironically, French pacifism made war all the more likely, since it encouraged Bismarck to believe that France would remain neutral. The Austrians, however, were not similarly convinced, especially after Napoleon fooled them into thinking that Prussia had promised him compensation in the Rhineland. With a knife held to their throat, as Metternich put it, in a secret treaty signed in Vienna on 12 June 1866, they finally agreed that, in the event of an Austrian victory in a war with Prussia, they would cede Venetia to France. In return France promised its own neutrality, and undertook to try to keep Italy neutral. The Austrians also gave a verbal pledge to countenance the creation of 'a new independent German state' in the Rhine provinces, should the war produce gains for the pro-Austrian, smaller German states of Saxony, Wurttemberg, and Bavaria. For France, that opened the way to an eventual annexation of the Rhineland.[8]

On the eve of the Austro-Prussian War, the French Emperor appeared to have negotiated himself into a strong position. It is doubtless an exaggeration to suggest that 'one word from Napoleon III would have preserved peace',[9] but he could feel confident enough to reject an appeal for neutrality from the Prussian king on the grounds that it contained insufficient guarantees of compensation for France. Bismarck, for all his supposed contempt for 'the sphynx of the Tuileries', as Metternich called him ('a sphynx without a secret' in Bismarck's view), continued to make last-minute bids for his support. Napoleon seemed set to benefit from an Austro-Prussian war whatever the outcome. In order to make his position clear to the French public, on 11 June he wrote an open letter to Drouyn which stated that France would remain neutral, but might have to intervene if the balance of power in Europe were to be upset. Had the war unfolded as anticipated, Napoleon III might well have deserved the title of arbiter of Europe, and been hailed as a new Talleyrand, if not a new Napoleon the Great. He envisaged an even contest, reckoning 'the Austrian army the better of the two – the Prussian the better appointed'.[10] What neither he nor anyone else foresaw was the defeat of Austria in a matter of weeks, and the revelation of a new and awesome great power in Europe. The might of the Prussian army swept away every illusion that the destiny of Europe could ever be decided from the Tuileries.

At first the war seemed to go as expected, with an Austrian victory over the Italians at Custozza on 24 June – a result which Napoleon considered would make the Italians more dependent than ever on his good will. But the Prussians were an altogether more formidable foe. In a drive across the plains of Bohemia, their army inflicted such damage on the Austrian army that by 1 July its commander, Benedek, had to ask Vienna for permission to sue for an armistice. He was ordered to fight on, but allowed to retreat, while his government hastily contacted Napoleon III to act as mediator. The Emperor delayed his reply for a day, until 3 July, when he agreed to make representations to Prussia and Italy if Austria would cede Venetia to him right away. At that very moment, however, the Austrian forces were capitulating at the battle of Sadowa.

The news reached Napoleon on the morning of 4 July, as he was preparing to go off to Vichy. It came as a considerable shock, and made him realise that, at the very least, he had underrated the power of the Prussian army. Yet he remained optimistic that the situation could be turned to his advantage. On the evening of 4 July, Metternich confirmed that Vienna accepted the terms he had stipulated for his mediation. Napoleon immediately telegraphed the Kings of Prussia and Italy, proposing himself as mediator, but he deliberately refrained from clarifying whether he meant to be an armed or a peaceful mediator. Armed intervention was certainly contemplated. A dispatch to Gramont, ambassador in Vienna, announced that France would join in on the Austrian side if the Emperor's mediation were refused. But, to reassure French public opinion, the *Moniteur* of 5 July published a statement informing the country that Venetia had been ceded to France and that Napoleon had offered his services as mediator to the Kings of Prussia and Italy. The announcement was greeted with an explosion of joy throughout the country, and the Emperor fêted as a master diplomat who had kept France at peace and still pulled off a striking coup.

All the while Napoleon was in a dilemma about how best to react to the extraordinary developments. His advisers gave him conflicting advice. At a council of ministers held on 5 July, he came under heavy pressure from Drouyn and the Empress to opt for military intervention. Marshal Randon assured him that 80,000 men could be mobilised immediately, and another 250,000 within three weeks. Magne and Persigny lent their voices to the pro-interventionist argument. La Valette, Minister of the Interior, led the opposition to such a move, on the grounds that the best interests of France resided in continuing to cultivate good relations with Prussia and Italy. Rouher and Baroche were of like mind. Napoleon gave no indication of his own position, but allowed the meeting to close with a decision to dispatch 50,000 men without delay to the Rhine frontier, along with a warning to Berlin spelling out French opposition to territorial change in Europe effected without the consent of France. It was also agreed that the Legislative Body should be asked to vote credits to permit a general mobilisation.[11]

Had Napoleon decided to go ahead with a show of force on the Rhine, the whole course of European history would have been altered. The question of how many men were available to be sent is misleading: as Randon said in his memoirs, a gathering of village policemen would have been enough to make Prussia pause.[12] Yet Napoleon hesitated to commit himself to an interventionist policy, and agonised over the most difficult decision he had yet had to take. Those of his entourage who favoured non-intervention continued to press their case. Both Rouher and La Valette returned to the Tuileries after the meeting, while Prince Napoleon also made strenuous representations against any alliance with the 'cadaver' of Austria against the more youthful and vigorous 'nationalistic' powers. Plon-Plon even took steps to contact Bismarck to assure him that there was no question of French action being taken against Prussia, and telegraphed his father-in-law, Victor Emmanuel, to advise him to reject the armistice proposal. Over the course of the night of 5-6 July, the Emperor made up his mind against an activist policy.[13]

A distinguished diplomatic historian has called non-intervention the 'great political error of the reign'.[14] That judgement remains accurate, for Napoleon III was pledged publicly to oppose any drastic alteration in the balance of power as a result of the Austro-Prussian War. No action of his could have prevented the emergence of Prussia as a military power of the front rank, but he could have resisted the creation of a new and powerful German state capable of posing a threat to French security. Accounts which attribute inaction to weakness on the part of the Emperor, however, are misleading. Explanations range from the onset of illness, to lack of confidence in the readiness of his troops, and an awareness that public opinion was overwhelmingly opposed to war. What all such speculations ignore is that in 1866, after much hesitation and consultation, Napoleon III consciously and deliberately set his face against war. To have sided with Austria would have been to renounce his 'Napoleonic ideas' and all his efforts to bring about changes in the European order. Prussia was the 'progressive' power, and might yet prove an ally in the process of revision. To make war on Prussia, and possibly also on Italy, would have been a repudiation of all his diplomatic endeavours, which had seemed to be on the point of bearing fruit before the news of Sadowa. To safeguard what had already been accomplished and to allow for future developments, the most prudent policy seemed to be to avoid war and to trust to diplomacy. Non-intervention, therefore, was the policy consistent with his general aims and not the product of any personal decline. With hindsight, one knows that he was wrong to place any faith in negotiations with Bismarck. That was less obvious at the time and, if anything, his mistake sprang from over-confidence rather than weakness. He gambled – and lost.

Having rejected armed intervention, Napoleon persisted with his attempts to mediate peacefully. King William of Prussia agreed in principle, but was evasive about what would constitute acceptable terms for an armistice. Victor Emmanuel was more intransigent. Unwilling to accept Venetia simply as a gift from France, and desperate to redeem Italian honour on the battlefield, he raised his demands to include not just Venetia but also the Tyrol and a solution to the Roman question. At a second meeting of the council of ministers, on 8 July, Napoleon once again considered the possibility of military intervention. In the case of Italy, it was ruled out, and Prince Napoleon was commissioned to treat directly with the Italian government. In the case of Prussia, it was kept as an option, though one increasingly unlikely to be used, especially after the arrival in Paris on 10 July of a special mission from Prussia, headed by Prince Reuss.

Napoleon was under no illusion that he was being strung along until Bismarck had devised his own peace terms, and his embarrassment was acute. Yet, when Drouyn made a last-ditch attempt to persuade him to change his mind at another meeting of the council, on 11 July, he continued to side with Rouher and Plon-Plon. The Emperor resigned himself to a say in the peace negotiations, while accepting that the agenda had to be set by the Prussian Minister-President. Bismarck manoeuvred with consummate skill, securing a less draconian settlement than his royal master would have liked. Even so, Napoleon was obliged to accept an outcome which provided for a far greater territorial enlargement of Prussia than he had originally been willing to concede. Prussia acquired 4 million new subjects, annexed from Hanover, Nassau, Hesse-Cassel and Frankfurt. Napoleon managed to negotiate the independence of Saxony and a pledge that the new North German Confederation should not extend south of the Main river. He also insisted that a plebiscite should be held in North Schleswig. Austria was to be excluded from the new Germany, though its territorial integrity, apart from Venetia, was guaranteed. Such were the terms which permitted a truce to come into force on 22 July, and a preliminary peace to be signed at Nikolsburg on 26 July. They were consolidated in the Treaty of Prague on 23 August 1866. Fighting between the Italians and the Austrians continued until 12 August, and a peace treaty was not concluded until October, when, after a plebiscite to determine the will of the local population, France transferred Venetia to Italy.

On the morrow of the 1866 war, Napoleon III could reflect that his actions had helped bring about some of the long-term goals which he had set himself. The former German Con-federation, a creation of the hated treaties of 1815, had been destroyed. The new German state which replaced it could be represented as a victory for the principle of nationality. Italy, whose very existence as a modern state owed much to French arms, was further indebted to his generosity for the acquisition of Venetia. On an optimistic assessment, Napoleon could hope for a new alignment of European forces centred on France, Prussia and Italy.

In reality, he had little justification for optimism. The events of 1866 dealt a lethal blow to Napoleon's power and prestige. The Austrians would not forget how he had abandoned them. The Italians were far from grateful for his machinations on their behalf, still harbouring unrequited nationalist ambitions, and preferring to believe that they had 'liberated' Venetia themselves after their army under General Cialdini entered the province on 8 July. The Prussians, confident in their own devastating military power, no longer needed to court or to fear the French Emperor. Russia, too, had cause to be aggrieved, having seen its suggestions for a congress on the German question rejected by France as well as Britain in early August. The new British Foreign Secretary, Lord Stanley, summed up Napoleon's uneasy situation:

> In 1859, he encouraged an Italian war, hoping to establish an Italian confederacy dependent on France. Instead of that he has created a strong united Italy, not even friendly to France. In 1866 he has allowed a German war to begin, hoping various results none of which has been obtained. He has created by the side of France a strong compact German empire fully the equal of France in military power. Was ever man so over-reached twice?[15]

A revolution in the balance of power had been effected, with the apparent compliance of France. Yet France itself had made no territorial gains. Marshal Randon's verdict was that 'it is we who were beaten at Sadowa'.[16] French public opinion largely agreed with him.

. . . . .

## 'COMPENSATIONS'

Public opinion was fickle. At the outset of the Austro-Prussian War it was strongly in favour of peace. By mid-July, it had changed sufficiently not to be the overriding argument against intervention. By the time of the Treaty of Prague, it was strongly anti-Prussian. No longer was the Emperor fêted as on 5 July, when he had seemed the all-powerful arbiter of Europe. Instead, there was growing indignation that France had stood idly by while a new and potentially hostile state had burst onto the European stage. In a letter of 20 July, former minister Magne warned him:

National sentiment would be deeply wounded, let there be no doubt about it, if in the end France should obtain by her intervention nothing but two nations attached to her flanks who had become dangerous by their exorbitantly increased power. Everybody says that greatness is a relative thing and that a country can be reduced while remaining the same when new forces increase around it.[17]

The solution seemed to be to seek territorial compensation for France. As early as 23 July, Napoleon had Benedetti make a bid for the French boundaries of 1814 and Luxembourg, but the ambassador came away empty-handed when Bismarck told him that, if France maintained the demand, he would not sign the Nikolsburg agreement. Between 28 July and 7 August, the Emperor was away in Vichy, seriously ill. To maintain control of policy, he appointed Rouher to handle foreign affairs alongside Drouyn, despite the fact that the two men had diametrically opposed views. Quite how decisions were taken in this period is not entirely clear, but, on 29 July, Benedetti received new instructions from Drouyn to approach Bismarck with a view to concluding a secret treaty with Prussia and to obtaining the Saar, the Bavarian Palatinate, Mainz and the demilitarisation of Luxembourg. Bismarck sent him packing, with a threat to oppose such demands with an army of 800,000 men. He then leaked details of the negotiations to the French press. When *Le Siècle* broke the news on 10 August, opinion at home was outraged at another humiliation, while foreign opinion was stirred by what appeared to be the dangerous ambitions of France. The south German states were particularly alarmed, and hastened to conclude the offensive–defensive alliance with Prussia that Bismarck wanted. Back in Paris, but still being treated for his difficulties in urinating, Napoleon was obliged to repudiate his foreign minister in an interview with Goltz on 11 August and, shortly afterwards, to accept Drouyn's resignation, even though the latter almost certainly had merely been carrying out his master's policy.

Having appointed La Valette interim foreign minister, pending the arrival of Moustier, ambassador at Constantinople, and having also assigned Rouher a role in the formulation of foreign policy, Napoleon proceeded to try to reassure the public about the French government's perspective on recent events. On 17 September 1866, the *Moniteur* published a circular, signed by La Valette but in fact prepared by Rouher in consultation with the Emperor himself, with assistance from the economist Michel Chevalier. The document claimed that the people of France had no need to be alarmed by the creation of a new Germany. Rather, they could be pleased at the shattering of the settlement of 1815 and the disappearance of 'the coalition of the three courts of the North'. Both the North German Confederation and the Kingdom of Italy could provide France with valuable new friends in a world where, increasingly, peoples would be grouped in larger agglomerations. Indeed, such developments in Europe were all the more desirable, given the likely rise in the power and influence of the United States and Russia – a remarkable prediction in 1866. France, recognising the positive side of the new trends, was declared to be not averse to enlargements of its own territory, provided these 'would not alter [its] powerful cohesion'. Here was more than a hint that Napoleon was interested in acquiring Luxembourg, Belgium and possibly part of Switzerland. In any case, the government could be relied upon to protect French interests. Hence, without intending a threat to anyone, it planned to sponsor a programme of far-reaching military reform.

The La Valette circular did little to restore confidence in Napoleon III's foreign policy. Had the public been aware of what was going on behind the scenes, it would have had even more cause for complaint. Napoleon had been persisting with his efforts to form an alliance with Prussia, but to no great avail. Bismarck, who might have been glad of a French alliance in 1865, had no need of one after Sadowa. Nevertheless, he did not at first give a flat refusal to the renewed overtures from Benedetti, preferring to imply that he might be interested if France were willing to pay a higher price; namely, to agree to the complete unification of Germany. Napoleon III had no more enthusiasm for a fully united Germany than he had for a fully united Italy, but, anxious to produce some territorial gain comparable with the acquisition of Nice and Savoy, he permitted Benedetti to submit to Bismarck a proposal, dated 29 August 1866, which accepted a further enlargement of Germany in return for German agreement to French acquisition of Luxembourg and, eventually, Belgium. Bismarck gave no direct reply to the approach. He did, however, retain the draft of the proposed treaty. In 1870, after the outbreak of the

Franco-Prussian War, he would publish it in *The Times* as evidence of French ambition.

Spurned in his efforts to conclude an alliance with Prussia, Napoleon pressed ahead with his plans for 'compensations', targeting Luxembourg in the first instance. The status of the duchy was complicated. Its Grand Duke was the King of the Netherlands, but, as a former member of the German Confederation, it still retained a garrison of Prussian troops. The population was partly French, partly German. Its ruler was in principle willing to sell to Napoleon III, provided Prussia made no objections. Bismarck showed no sign of being opposed to the deal when Napoleon first broached it with him in early 1867. Only when negotiations between France and Luxembourg had reached an advanced stage did he decide to intervene, announcing in the Reichstag on 1 April that the transfer of Luxembourg to France, without the consultation of both the great powers and the German people, was unacceptable. Bismarck's statement was all the more unwelcome because it came hard on the heels of his revelation, in March 1867, of the existence of the offensive–defensive alliance between Prussia and the other German states, which shattered Rouher's claims in parliament that the new order in Germany was more favourable than previously to French interests, because of the tripartite division into the North German Confederation, South Germany and Austria.

At the threat of war, the Grand Duke hastily backed out of the arrangement with France, leaving Napoleon in yet another difficult situation. Once again Prussia was the obstacle to the 'compensations' he felt he needed, and for several days he seriously contemplated going to war, abandoning the idea only because of France's lack of allies, and because his projected military reforms had not yet been put through. Nevertheless, national honour and the security of the dynasty required some face-saving operation. Moustier therefore demanded that the Prussian garrison should be withdrawn from Luxembourg. Alarmed that this demand might provide the occasion for war, Great Britain stepped in with a proposal for an international congress to be held in London, which met between 28 April and 7 May 1867. Prussia backed down, but only in return for the neutralisation of Luxembourg, along the lines of Belgium and Switzerland. Peace was preserved, but France had lost its last

chance of 'compensation'. And the growing antagonism between France and Prussia had been intensified.

* * * *

## THE ROMAN QUESTION

Napoleon's vulnerability was highlighted by continuing reverses
in foreign policy. Even his successes went sour, as in the case of
the Roman question. The Convention of September 1864, providing for the troop withdrawal which he had been seeking for
so long, appeared to be a triumph for his diplomacy, but
immediately gave rise to difficulties when it became known that
Florence rather than Rome had secretly been envisaged as the
capital of the new Italy. Italian nationalists were determined on
Rome, while French conservatives denounced any further sell-
out of the papacy. A difficult situation was aggravated by Pius
IX's encyclical *Quanta Cura* (8 December 1864), attached to
which was a *Syllabus of Errors* condemning as heretical propositions dear to the contemporary liberal conscience. Notably, it
defended the temporal power and anathematised the notion
that 'the Roman pontiff should reconcile and align himself with
progress, liberalism and modern civilisation'. Napoleon III's
government protested at theses which appeared to challenge its
authority, and at first tried to prevent publication of the *Syllabus*.
Having failed, (the terms of the *Syllabus* were expounded from
the pulpit), it decided to publicise the text with a view to
arousing general indignation. In this calculation at least the
government was not mistaken.

The problem was that, subsequent to the evacuation of
troops as planned, between December 1865 and December
1866, no satisfactory arrangement could be found to guarantee
the sovereignty of the Pope in the territory that remained to
him. In December 1866, Napoleon tried yet again to hold a
great power conference on the Roman question, this time by
enlisting the support of Prussia. His hopes had been raised by
the enthusiasm of the Prussian envoy to Rome, Count Harry
Arnim von Suchow, but Bismarck refused to enter into any
Franco-Prussian agreement regarding the temporal power. On
the contrary, the German Chancellor enjoyed the spectacle of
French embarrassment over Rome, and had no intention of
allowing the French Emperor to trap him into a course of action
which could detach Prussia from its Italian ally. The Pope

therefore continued to be subject to assaults, like that launched by Garibaldi's followers in October 1867. Napoleon was obliged to threaten the Italian government with the return of French troops because of its own reluctance to act against a national hero, and made good his threat by sending French reinforcements to the papal army. Together, on 3 November 1867 at Mentana, they inflicted a crushing defeat on the Garibaldians. The Emperor derived little satisfaction from this victory for French arms. As he told Lord Clarendon: 'I have had to make this expedition *against my will* [my italics], but I couldn't do otherwise because every French pulpit would have become a rostrum attacking me.'[18]

French troops were to remain stationed in Rome until the end of the Second Empire. The expedition, so lightly undertaken in 1849, turned out to be not the least of the factors which contributed to Napoleon's eventual downfall.

. . .

## MORE SETBACKS

After 1867, Napoleon III abandoned the pursuit of a dynamic foreign policy and settled rather for a defence of the status quo. Having devoted most of his public life to the destruction of the old concert of Europe established in 1815, he now embraced the idea of a new concert committed to maintaining the European order which had been established by the Treaty of Prague. Austria, formerly his foremost enemy, was wooed as an ally with a similar interest in preventing further change. In August 1867, Napoleon met with Francis Joseph at Salzburg, and both emperors declared their resolve to uphold the existing balance of power. Ideally, Napoleon wanted France and Austria to convoke a European congress 'which would consecrate the present status quo, limiting it to boundaries determined upon together'. For Napoleon, such a congress would have the double merit of checking further expansion on the part of Prussia and of allaying the fears of public opinion in France. As a sign of how far his thinking had evolved, he expressed his readiness to see the congress gather at ... Vienna![19]

As usual, Napoleon communicated his thoughts to the French public through a pamphlet, '*Congrès ou la guerre*'. The Austrians, fearful of provoking Prussia, were unenthusiastic, and countered with their own proposals for disarmament, which found little favour with either the French or the British. The Prussians, nor surprisingly, vehemently opposed the idea of a congress the principal objective of which was to curb their power. By the end of 1868, Napoleon had to recognise that yet another of his congress schemes had come to nothing. Likewise, his hopes of concluding an alliance with Austria remained unrealised. The Luxembourg affair had convinced Napoleon of the need for a closer association of the two powers, even to the point of an offensive–defensive alliance, by which, in the event of successful war against Prussia, France would take the left bank of the Rhine while Austria would regain Silesia and reassert its position *vis-à-vis* the German states. The Austrians, however, were not to be seduced. All too painfully aware of Prussian power in Germany, they preferred to accept the verdict of 1866 and to redirect their ambitions towards the Balkans (a tendency reinforced by the internal reorganisation of the Empire into the Dual Monarchy of Austria-Hungary, for the Hungarians were more antagonistic towards Russia than towards Prussia). Not wishing to alienate Russia completely by favouring Austrian designs in the Balkans, Napoleon had to settle for a vague *entente* with Austria.

In early January 1869 he tried a new ploy: a triple alliance of France, Austria and Italy, to be followed by a European congress. The carrot dangled before Austria was the security of not having to worry about an Italian attack on the Trentino, while the Italians might hope to secure that region, along with Rome, by negotiation rather than by force. Rome, indeed, was rapidly indicated as the price of Italy's compliance in the triple alliance scheme, given the hostility aroused in Italy by Mentana and the rash promise made by Rouher in the French Legislative Body on 16 March 1867 'never' to concede Italian claims to the Eternal City. Napoleon still balked at paying such a price, and though the eventual prospect of a triple alliance was not ruled out altogether, it had been dropped as an immediate prospect by September 1869. The goal of securing a Franco-Austrian alliance continued to elude the French Emperor.

He did, however, succeed in convening a conference in January 1869, when the Eastern Question once again flared up in the form of a dispute between Greece and Turkey over Crete. Napoleon proposed mediation of the powers, less because of any genuine concern with the quarrel at issue but more because of his obsession with the German problem and the desirability of bringing the concert of Europe together to confirm its commitment to the status quo. Napoleon hoped that the conference, which met in Paris, might set a precedent for the resolution of international disputes without war, and thus thwart Prussian ambitions in southern Germany. Unfortunately for him, no other power interpreted the conference in that light.

There remained the possibility of doing some sort of deal with Russia. Back in December 1866, Napoleon had hinted that he would not be averse to seeing a further dismemberment of the Ottoman Empire (in the specific instance of Crete) if Russia would make a firm commitment to France. The Tsar was unwilling to give such an undertaking, and – with that cynicism and opportunism which were the hallmarks of his diplomacy – Napoleon promptly reverted to his posture of upholding the integrity of the Turkish Empire so as not to lose favour with Britain. The Russians had continued to draw closer to Prussia, and in March 1868 entered into a secret agreement whereby they promised to mobilise on the Austrian frontier should Prussia find itself at war with France. Napoleon was unaware of this agreement when he dispatched his favourite general, Fleury, to be ambassador in St Petersburg, charged with a mission to sound out Russian opinion regarding a *rapprochement*. He discovered that Russia's aims were still to revise the Treaty of Paris, and the negotiations foundered.

At the end of his reign, Napoleon's diplomacy seemed to be blocked at every turn. The days of glory were long since past, and, in a dangerous world, France found itself without firm friends. In the first half of 1870, he conducted secret conversations with Austrian military leaders, but again without concluding an alliance. Italy, too, was deaf to his overtures while Rome remained under the protection of French troops. British statesmen, always suspicious of Napoleon's goals, had their convictions reinforced by his role in the affair of the Belgian railways. The latter involved a quarrel between France and Belgium over the French government's financial backing for a commercial agreement between the French Compagnie des Chemins de Fer de l'Est and two Belgian railroad companies. The deal gave the French the right to operate two lines of considerable strategic and economic significance, linking France, Belgium, Holland and Luxembourg, and the Brussels government stepped in to impose a veto on the grounds that it might constitute a violation of Belgian neutrality, which would arouse the ire of Berlin. Riled by what was widely believed to be yet another rebuff at the hands of Prussia, Napoleon reacted vehemently, even threatening to make war on Belgium. This in turn triggered a strong British response, which included a mobilisation of the Channel fleet. After a good deal of bluster on the part of French foreign minister La Valette, France backed down, and the affair was settled in July 1869 by having the lines placed under international control. Once again, Napoleon ended up looking both a loser and a fomentor of discord. Well before the disaster of 1870, the image of the Emperor as a master diplomat had been badly tarnished, and his failures in the field of foreign policy had begun to put him under increasing pressure from the opposition in France.

. . .

## NOTES AND REFERNCES

1. On Bismarck, see Gall L 1986 *Bismarck: the White Revolutionary*, 2 vols, Allen & Unwin (in particular, vol 1, p. 132)
2. Quoted by Bury J P T 1964 *Napoleon III and the Second Empire*. English Universities Press, p. 112
3. Bernstein P 1971 'Napoleon III and Bismarck: the Biarritz–Paris Talks of 1865', in Barker N N and Brown M L (eds) *Diplomacy in an Age of Nationalism: Essays in Honor of Lynn Marshall Case*. Martinus Nijhoff, pp. 124–43
4. *Historical Dictionary of the French Second Empire 1852–1870*. Echard W E (ed) 1985, Greenwood Press
5. Pottinger E A 1966 *Napoleon III and the German Crisis 1865–1866*. Harvard University Press
6. Bush J W 1967 *Venetia Redeemed: Franco-Italian Relations 1864–1866*. Syracuse University Press, pp. 68ff
7. Case L 1954 *French Opinion on War and Diplomacy during the Second Empire*. University of Pennsylvania Press, p. 202
8. Bush 1967, p. 55
9. Mosse W E 1958 *European Powers and the German Question 1848–1871: with Special Reference to England and Russia*. Cambridge University Press, p. 238
10. Corley T A B 1961 *Democratic Despot: a Life of Napoleon III*, Barrie & Rockliff, p. 275
11. Pottinger 1966, p. 156ff
12. Randon J L C A 1875–77, *Mémoires du Maréchal Randon*, 2 vols, vol 2, p. 146

13. Pottinger 1966, pp. 160–1
14. Renouvin P 1940 *La politique extérieure du Second Empire.* Mimeograph, Cours de Sorbonne
15. Quoted by Mosse 1958, p. 241
16. Randon *Mémoires* vol 2, p. 145
17. Text in *Papiers et correspondance de la famille impériale* 1870–72, 2 vols, vol 1, pp. 238ff
18. Case 1954, p. 171
19. Echard W E 1983 *Napoleon III and the Concert of Europe.* Louisiana State University, p. 280

*Chapter 8*

# THE PRESSURES OF POWER
## (1864–70)

A perceptible change could be detected in the political atmosphere in France after the setbacks to Napoleon III's diplomacy during the political crisis of 1863. The Emperor shed much of the aura of success which had surrounded his dealings with foreign powers, and critics of the regime became increasingly strident in their opposition. The Belgian diplomat Baron Beyens sensed 'a vague feeling of fear and a widespread unease that once again the French were "on the threshold of great unknown events"'. As he put it, 'on every side I hear repeated: "if we are not at 1847 we are at least at 1845"'.[1] It would be wrong to assume that the Second Empire was already doomed, and that its downfall in 1870 could already have been predicted at the end of 1863. The military débâcle which eventually swept the regime away took most observers by surprise. Nevertheless, it was already clear to intelligent commentators that changes were on the way on the domestic political front as much as on the international scene. Continuing reverses abroad inevitably gave rise to discontent at home, and convinced Napoleon that new measures were required to stem the clamour of opposition. After the elections of 1863, around forty deputies had begun to constitute themselves into a 'third party', a group animated by the liberal Orleanist Louis Buffet, but composed largely of Bonapartists keen to see a further liberalisation of the regime. It included also a number of clericals and protectionists, along with independents like Emile Ollivier, now increasingly detached from his former republican colleagues. Thiers, though not formally a member of the group, was a collaborator, lending his voice to the demand for the return of parliamentary government. In a famous speech in January 1864, he demanded the restoration of 'the necessary freedoms', as we have seen. In

March 1866, Ollivier moved an amendment against the address to the throne, which obtained forty-two signatures. Its purpose was to urge Napoleon III to continue with the reforms begun in 1860, and, though it was defeated by 206 votes to 63, in the course of the debate the 'Vice-Emperor', Rouher, was obliged to concede that further reform would be forthcoming at an appropriate moment.

. . .

## MORE LIBERALISATION

Napoleon had always said that he was willing to restore political liberties when the time was right. In February 1853, he had declared that 'liberty has never helped to found a lasting political edifice: it crowns the edifice when time has consolidated it'.[2] Precisely what the Emperor meant by liberty, however, is difficult to determine. His own leanings were always authoritarian, and he had little faith in ministerial responsibility or freedom of the press. Perhaps Prince Napoleon's formula – 'progress towards liberty through dictatorship' – sums up also the position of his cousin the Emperor. In December 1866, Napoleon used Walewski to sound out Ollivier as to whether he would be prepared to accept a place in a 'liberal' cabinet designed to represent 'the crowning of the edifice'. Ollivier soon discovered that Napoleon had only limited concessions in mind. He was prepared to permit deputies the right to question ministers on policy, but baulked at conceding ministerial responsibility, complete freedom of the press and of public meetings, and the end to government interference in elections, which Ollivier also demanded. Only Napoleon's need to repair the damage to his prestige in the aftermath of Sadowa and the Mexican disaster persuaded him to go forward with reform.

On 19 January 1867, the *Moniteur* unexpectedly announced a package of liberal measures. Interpellation of ministers was to be introduced, and legislation on the right to hold public meetings and on freedom of the press was promised for the near future. No one was deceived that the reforms were anything other than pure opportunism on Napoleon's part, designed to win back the political initiative. The apparent shift towards liberalism still refused the principle of ministerial responsibility and was accompanied by no changes in his ministerial team. On the contrary, while the likes of Rouher, Baroche and Fould remained at their posts, with the active connivance of the Empress, they did all in their power to hamper the progress of reform. Rouher was the key obstacle. Having blocked the appointment of Ollivier as *rapporteur* for the projected press law, in March 1867 he launched a vitriolic attack on Walewski and ousted him from the presidency of the Legislative Body. It was thanks to him, too, that the press law, aimed at ending government interference in the starting up and running of newspapers, was delayed until 11 May 1868. In consequence, the reform appeared less a concession from above than one extorted from below. The limited nature of the measures of January 1867 was a particular disappointment to Ollivier, who, ending his flirtations with the regime, returned to vigorous opposition. In a speech of 12 July 1867, he denounced Rouher as the Emperor's 'evil genius', a 'grand vizier', a 'mayor of the palace' and a 'vice-emperor'.[3] Napoleon, despite his regard for Ollivier, had no choice but to back his minister, and immediately rewarded him with the Grand Cross of the Legion of Honour. The Emperor was still not prepared to establish the 'liberal Empire' that Ollivier and others wanted.

. . .

## THE FAILURE OF REFORM

Nevertheless, the degree to which Napoleon III's position had deteriorated was apparent not just in the clamour for political change but in the Emperor's inability to reform both the educational system and the army along his preferred lines. Victor Duruy, his able and anticlerical Education Minister since 1863, was keen to help Napoleon bring in free, and in due course compulsory, primary education, which provoked opposition not just from 'clerical' deputies in parliament but also from a number of his ministerial colleagues. Duruy did succeed in improving the material conditions of schoolteachers, and he was also one of the pioneers of courses in adult education. Another lasting achievement was the founding of the Ecole Pratique des Hautes Etudes. What sparked off the greatest rumpus, however, was his attempt in 1867 to establish secondary courses for girls to be given by male teachers from the Sorbonne and the boys' *lycées*. Intended as an attack on clerical control of girls' secondary education (Duruy claimed that 'we have left this education in the hands of people who are neither of their time nor of their country'), the courses met with resolute hostility on the part of the Catholic clergy. Bishop Dupanloup, who led the campaign, complained that Duruy wanted to detach women from the Church and, worse, had revealed himself to be a Darwinist 'who saw man as a perfected orang-outang'. Bowing to clerical pressure, Napoleon was obliged to accept Duruy's resignation in July 1869.[4]

The failure of army reform was even more striking – and ultimately fatal to the survival of the regime. In the wake of Sadowa, no one appreciated the need for military reorganisation better than the Emperor. The basic problem was the system of conscription. Under the Soult law of 1832, 150,000 men aged twenty were, in theory, called up every year. In practice, it was the legislature which decided annually on the number to be enlisted (the *contingent*). During the Empire, the *contingent* usually averaged around 100,000 men, which dispensations reduced to around 80,000. Since there were always more twenty-year-old youths than places available in the army, the custom was to draw lots to decide which of them should serve. Conscripts were the holders of a 'bad number', though here again it was possible for a man with the means to hire someone else to replace him. The net result was that, instead of the force of 1 million men envisaged by the Soult law, the army in peacetime consisted of between 320,000 and 420,000 men, most of them hardened professionals rather than conscripts. During the Italian war of 1859, Napoleon had witnessed at first hand the dangers which could arise from the lack of a trained reserve. Sadowa convinced him of the superiority of the Prussian system, which could mobilise 750,000 men on account of the time which conscripts spent not only on active service but in the *Landswehr*.

In August 1866, the Emperor set in train a plan for the introduction of a similar scheme in France, with a view to being able to raise an army of 1 million men. The military chiefs, headed by Randon, were distinctly unenthusiastic, preferring an army of professionals to one which was dependent on reserves. On 31 October, with the Emperor as president, a commission was set up to examine France's military options, but it failed to produce a scheme which commanded the assent of all its members. Frustrated, Napoleon disbanded the commission and sacked Randon, replacing him at the War Office with Marshal Niel in January 1867. Between them, Napoleon and Niel elaborated a new plan which envisaged that those who drew a *mauvais numéro* would serve for five years in the active army and three in the reserves, while those with a *bon numéro* would do three years in the reserves, followed by five years in a new force, the *garde mobile*, a kind of militia which could be called upon to serve, and to maintain order, in wartime. All who were exempted from military service for whatever reason would also spend some time in the *garde mobile*, with the happy consequence that France would have introduced a genuinely universal form of conscription, capable of putting 1 million men in the field.

Niel's project met with a chorus of abuse. Republicans, suspicious (not without reason) of a standing army in peacetime, called for the abolition of the professional army, and its replacement with a citizen army. Orleanists were likewise fearful of the potential for 'despotism' inherent in the proposals, and objected also to the removal of parliamentary control over the size of the *contingent*. Middle-class families were outraged at the prospect both of being denied the right to buy exemptions from service for their sons and of having to pay higher taxes to support a larger army. Peasants preferred to take their chance under the lottery system, since that left them with at least the possibility of being exempted. The military themselves continued to favour a hard-core professional army. Napoleon was willing to submit Niel's bill to the verdict of the electorate, but was dissuaded by Rouher, who let him know the strength of feeling in the country. Even in the more 'patriotic' eastern part of France, it seemed, the population which had been clamouring for war at the time of Sadowa was not willing to shoulder the burden of defence. To a degree, the government was a victim of its own propaganda. If, as it repeatedly claimed, the new order in Europe contained no special danger to France, why was there any need for expensive army reform?

Replying to the latter argument, Napoleon told the Legislative Body when it reconvened in February 1867 that

> a nation's influence depends on the number of men she can put under arms. Do not forget that neighbouring states accept much heavier sacrifice for the good constitution of their armies and their eyes are fixed on you to see whether by your decisions the influence of France should increase or diminish in the world.[5]

His warnings fell on deaf ears. Petitions arrived from all over

France (especially from the west and the centre) to reinforce the reservations of the deputies. In March, Napoleon and Niel submitted a much revised bill (the reserve army was not to be trained and was to be called up only in wartime), but even this was too much for the legislature which, over the next ten months, amended the bill beyond recognition. The so-called *loi Niel* which was eventually voted in January 1868 bore no resemblance to the Emperor's original plan, being only a slight variation on the *loi Soult*. The one new provision was for the creation of a mobile national guard, but this was never set up, because of inadequate funding. In the end, not only did Napoleon fail to obtain the trained reserve and expert general staff which he had desired, but, in the process, he managed to stir up alarm and resentment all over France, thereby contributing to the already rising current of political opposition.

## THE MOUNTING CHALLENGE

Opposition to the Empire had never entirely ceased, but the easing of press restrictions and the restoration of the right to hold public meetings allowed it to manifest itself to an unprecedented degree. In the run-up to the 1869 elections, some 150 newspapers were founded, 120 of them hostile to the regime. The most vituperative was *La Lanterne*, the organ of Henri Rochefort. 'France', he proclaimed, 'has thirty-six million subjects, not counting the subjects of discontent.'[6] His favourite Bonaparte he declared to be Napoleon II, who had neither engaged in futile wars nor in distant and expensive adventures.

Republican organisations began to sprout everywhere. Some were run by old 48ers, but others flourished under the direction of a younger generation of republicans, many of whom were marked by the spirit of positivism and were militantly anticlerical. A number, following Gambetta, called also for more far-reaching social reform. From the time of the 1863 elections, republicans had devoted much of their energy towards capturing power at the municipal level, especially in the larger towns. After 1868, conditions were again favourable to campaigning at the national level. In addition to capitalising on the freedom of the press, they established electoral committees which, while relying essentially on local organisers (often drawn from the freemasons' lodges), benefited also from the guidance of nationally known figures such as Jules Favre and Gambetta. The latter, in particular, assumed the role of a national leader, presenting himself to the working-class electors of northern and eastern Paris in his 'Belleville programme' as a passionate opponent of 'Caesarian democracy' and the champion of radical republicanism.

The elections of May–June 1869 unleashed pent-up political passions. The government tried to maintain the system of official candidatures, but many prefects and mayors were reluctant to cooperate. In the towns, the system broke down under the sheer weight of opposition. In Paris the electoral campaign was accompanied by an upsurge in violence and threats to public order. Attendance at electoral meetings averaged 20,000 nightly, and rioting was commonplace. 333 candidates contested the nine seats in the capital, testifying to the heightened degree of politicisation. The government of the Second Empire faced an unprecedented challenge to its authority, and the results confirmed the fear of its most diehard supporters. In a poll of around eight million electors, government candidates won only 4.5 million votes, while opposition candidates polled 3.5 million. Between 1863 and 1869, the opposition's share of the vote had risen by 15 per cent (from 25 per cent to 40 per cent). By any reckoning, it was a poor show for a regime which had set out to represent national unity and to eliminate political divisions.

On the other hand, the results were hardly a victory for republicanism. Out of 292 seats, republicans won only 25. 'Liberal' opponents of the empire fared much better, winning some forty-nine seats. The great majority of the returned deputies (216) were Bonapartists, though only 118 had been 'official' candidates, with ninety-eight classifiable as 'pro-government' liberals. The countryside, once again, had shown itself to be overwhelmingly Bonapartist. Republicanism was strong only in the towns. The election results were a defeat both for irreconcilable republicans and for hardline Bonapartists, the 'mamelukes', who could muster, at best, about eighty deputies in the new Legislative Body. The real victors of the 1869 elections were the 'centrists' – that is, liberals, whether dynastic or 'opposition' (opponents of authoritarianism prepared to collaborate with a 'liberal' Empire). The new configuration of parliamentary power presented Napoleon III with new and trickier problems in the art of political survival. It has to be said that he rose to the occasion. His solution was to concede, at last, the 'liberal Empire'.

. . .

## A LIBERAL EMPEROR?

At first, the sensational election results encouraged speculation in the press that the end of the Empire might be in sight, and France on the brink of yet another revolution. Foreign tourists made haste to leave Paris, where the victories of the left were immediately greeted with demonstrations and violence on the streets. Ugly clashes between demonstrators and the police took place each night between 7 and 10 June, leading to over 1,000 arrests. Napoleon's response on 11 June was to drive through the city in an open carriage, with the Empress by his side. His appearance did not prevent another riot the same night, but it did signal that he had no intention of giving in to pressure from the streets. Napoleon III may have been 'a man prematurely aged' and 'painfully ill', but he was not 'hopelessly bewildered by events at home and abroad'.[7] On 16 June he published an open letter affirming his determination to stand firm in the face of threats and violence, and proceeded to appoint a nominee of Rouher to the vice-presidency of the Legislative Body.

Yet, despite the public bravado, he realised that some concessions were necessary. The new parliament was not due to meet until November, but Napoleon decided to convoke an extraordinary session to discover its will, and thus be in a stronger position to plan his own next move. On 6 July, 116 deputies, members of the 'third party' and liberal Bonapartists, indicated their support for an interpellation of the government designed to bring about ministerial responsibility. The 116 did not include republicans and monarchists, with whose additional support the government could have been defeated in the chamber. Napoleon, wishing to avoid the interpellation, agreed to change. On 12 July, Rouher announced his resignation to the Legislative Body and read out a statement from the Emperor promising a series of reforms to be submitted to the Senate, which included the right of the legislature to elect its own officers and to devise its own rules: extensions of the right to amend legislation and to question ministers: the right of ministers to be simultaneously deputies or senators: enlargement of the role of the Senate: and the possibility of tariff reform.

Napoleon then prorogued the Legislative Body and appointed an interim government under the marquis de Chasseloup-Laubat to implement the reforms by *senatus-consultum*. Chasseloup, formerly Minister of the Navy and of the Colonies, maintained the liberal momentum and drew up a programme which went beyond the liberties promised by the Emperor, adding a role for the legislature in the initiation of legislation and in the approval of international treaties concerning tariffs, and granting the Senate delaying power of up to one year over legislation. Passed on 8 September by *senatus-consultum*, the package marked an important step towards the return of parliamentary government.

Significantly, however, Napoleon III did not concede the principle of ministerial responsibility. Ministers remained 'dependent solely on the Emperor' (Article 2), even if they were also 'responsible'. The Emperor also retained the right to dissolve the legislature and to appeal directly to the people by plebiscite. Moreover, the Senate retained its constituent power. The constitution of 1852 was not abolished. Even after the elections of 1869, Napoleon III did not turn himself into a full-fledged 'liberal' emperor.

While these events were unfolding, Napoleon himself was stricken by his old bladder troubles. From mid-August, he was in pain and deprived of sleep. He could have taken little comfort from the fate of Marshal Niel, who had likewise developed a bladder stone, and died on 13 August after what was believed to have been a botched operation. Napoleon's illness prevented him from accompanying Eugénie to Corsica for the celebrations being held for his uncle's centenary. Rumours spread that the Emperor was dying, precipitating panic on the Bourse and fears of a red uprising. It was only in mid-September that he began to recover and to resume control of policy.

With his customary caution, Napoleon worked to put together a ministerial team which would be acceptable to both himself and the legislature when it met in November. The man he now wanted as his chief minister was the former republican Emile Ollivier, whom Morny had earlier talent-spotted as someone to rally support for a liberal Empire. Negotiations between the Emperor and Ollivier began in October and continued for the rest of the year. The exchanges included a clandestine evening meeting at Compiègne, at which Ollivier arrived in disguise. The two men sipped tea together, while Ollivier laid down his terms, which were to have the right to choose his own ministerial team and to implement his own programme. Napoleon continued to baulk at the idea of having a genuine prime minister answerable to parliament rather than to himself. Also, though he liked Ollivier, he was not convinced that, for all his idealism and oratorical skills, he possessed the requisite personal qualities to impose himself as a head of government. Their interview terminated without precise issue.

However, as Ollivier knew, the Emperor could not afford to hesitate for too long, for the political situation continued to deteriorate. On 22 November, a by-election in Paris returned the exiled Rochefort to the Legislative Assembly. Napoleon allowed him to take his seat. The country was also in the grip of a wave of strikes which had begun in June and had produced incidents like that at Aubin, where fourteen workers were killed. The meeting of the workers' International at Basle, and of the Congress of Liberty at Lausanne, likewise inspired fears of red revolution. Violent press attacks on the Emperor continued unabated. Napoleon appreciated that he had little choice but to go down the road of reform, and that Ollivier was the man best equipped to help him survive. The authoritarian figures were descredited, as even Persigny was prepared to admit. The Orleanists were distasteful to him. Having begun his tenure of power surrounded by the 'rue de Poitiers' clique, he had no intention of finishing that way: hence his shunning of the ambitious and masterful Thiers. The forty-four-year-old Ollivier seemed his best bet, despite his lack of a party and his being a man more respected than liked. On 27 December, he wrote to Ollivier to ask him to form a homogeneous cabinet which would adequately represent the majority in the Legislative Body.

Ollivier's commission was not without difficulty. From the end of November, the 'third party' had shown signs of an internal split, as a group of around thirty deputies became more intransigent, upping its demands to include further constitutional changes and the election of mayors. On 2 January 1870, however, he was able to put together a ministry composed of 'third party' members, a minority of the new 'centre-left' group and a couple of nominees of the Emperor himself. While Ollivier himself enjoyed his second honeymoon, the 'liberal Empire' came into existence.

The new chief minister was nothing if not self-confident. 'Sire', he declared solemnly, 'I am happy because I am saving your dynasty.'[8] Lord Clarendon took a less sanguine view, noting that his 'task requires tact, experience, firmness, knowledge of men, and a few other qualities in which he seems singularly deficient'.[9] Napoleon himself was more optimistic, since he believed that his own was still the controlling hand on the government. He observed:

> Ollivier has talent. He is young and may go far if properly guided. He has two precious qualities which make me forget his failings. He believes in me and is the eloquent interpreter of my ideas, especially when I let him think they are his own.[10]

Nevertheless, the new government faced an uphill struggle.

Reform was placed at the top of the political agenda. Legislation was henceforth to be based on proposals put forward by experts, on the model of English Royal Commissions. Government was to be decentralised, with self-government introduced in Paris. The role of the state in education was to be re-examined, along with the country's need for technical education. Public works and communications were also to be studied, while another commission, presided over by Ollivier himself, was to reform the penal code. Influenced by the ideas of Frédéric Le Play, Ollivier was keen to establish a permanent commission of 'social peace' conceived as a kind of arbitration body made up of workers, employers and experts. It was one thing, however, to have commissions make recommendations, and another for government to implement them. When the commission on decentralisation proposed that mayors should be elected, Napoleon III adamantly maintained his right to appoint them himself from the ranks of the municipal counsellors. Nor were parliamentarians happy to see their role in legislation diminished by Ollivier's experts. In addition, pending the reports of the commissions, reform remained a paper accomplishment, allowing Ollivier's critics to claim that the advent of the liberal Empire had not changed anything.

The charge was unfair. A number of liberal laws were passed, notably the repeal of the general security law of 1858. The press law was modified to permit offenders to be tried by jury. As a sign of the government's commitment to ending administrative interference in politics, twelve prefects were sacked, while Haussmann, the autocratic and unpopular Prefect of the Seine, resigned on the pretext that he could not serve 'under the flabby regime of a parliamentary empire'.[11] Restrictions on the foreign press were raised. Ledru-Rollin, finally, was pardoned. So, too, were some of the ringleaders of the recent strikes.

The government's credibility was also boosted by its firm stance in the Victor Noir affair. On 10 January 1870, Pierre Bonaparte, son of Napoleon's brother Lucien and the Emperor's cousin, killed a journalist called Victor Noir. The latter was one of Rochefort's collaborators, and had called at Prince Pierre's house in connection with a duel between Pierre and Rochefort over the journalist's anti-Bonapartist remarks in his newspaper *La Marseillaise*. Orchestrated by the left, Noir's funeral on 12 July was turned into a massive demonstration against the Empire. Rochefort himself, seeking to exploit the affair to the full, wrote a particularly inflammatory piece in his newspaper, declaring that he had been 'weak-minded enough to believe that a Bonaparte could be something other than a murderer'.[12] Ollivier, who had been quick to demand the arrest and trial of Prince Pierre, was equally decisive in mobilising the army to maintain order on the streets and in removing the parliamentary immunity of Rochefort to allow him to be prosecuted for insulting the Emperor and the imperial family. Pierre Bonaparte was tried at a special court in Tours, which acquitted him. Rochefort was given a six-months' prison sentence and fined 3,000 francs. The left, indignant at the contrasting fates of Prince Pierre and of Rochefort and Noir, again clashed on the streets with the forces of order. Ollivier, for his part, made no secret of his determination to uphold the authority of the government and to dampen down revolutionary agitation.

Indeed, the 'liberal' Empire had by no means abandoned all the methods of the 'authoritarian' Empire where 'order' was at stake. The same tough attitude was adopted towards striking steelworkers at Le Creusot, twenty-five of whom were arrested. Leaders of the First International, such as Varlin, the future *communard*, were also detained in custody. The police were accused of rampaging through the Latin Quarter, making indiscriminate attacks on bystanders. Despite Ollivier's commitment to freedom of the press, newspapers were prosecuted for attacks on the Emperor and 'insults to religion'. In justifying such repression, Ollivier insisted that liberty must never be confused with licence. The extremism of certain elements on the left gave rise to yet another 'red scare', especially in the countryside (where it was fanned by big landowners), and among the northern bourgeoisie. The polarisation of politics which had done so much to bring the Empire into being was resurfacing in the late 1860s, and looked set to perpetuate the regime as the only alternative to disorder.

Ollivier's most serious difficulties were with parliament. The Senate, presided over by Rouher, was ready to thwart his reforms, and rejected as unconstitutional his bill on the election of mayors. In retaliation, a sizeable number of deputies in the Legislative Body called for the complete abandonment of the 1852 constitution. Napoleon was unenthusiastic about constitutional change, but he allowed it to proceed. On 21 March 1870, Ollivier initiated a *senatus-consultum* to provide a new constitution which would recognise that constituent power resided in the people, not in the Senate, and which gave the two houses of parliament equal rights in the framing of legislation. On 28 March the project was submitted to the Senate, and after extensive debate, voted unanimously on 20 April 1870.

The new constitution which emerged from these proceedings was a strange mixture, even by the standards of nineteenth-century France.[13] The Emperor was proclaimed the head of the government, responsible to the French people, to whom he could appeal by plebiscite. Henceforth, however, he was bound to regard ministers and deputies not as his 'instruments' but as collaborators in the work of government. He also lost his right to be the sole initiator of legislation, since both houses of parliament were now given rights in this area. Ministers were declared to be 'responsible', but it was not stated to whom: the Emperor, or parliament, or both. Effectively, the constitution was the muddy sort of compromise which well suited the Emperor's determination to resist checks on his power. In the last resort, he could always appeal over the heads of the politicians to the people. And that, on the advice of Rouher, is precisely what he proceeded to do in May 1870, with the objective of reaffirming his personal authority.

The moment was propitious, given the mounting fear of disorder. On 8 May, adult males in the French population were asked to vote 'yes' or 'no' to the proposition: 'The people approve of the liberal reforms brought about in the Constitution since 1860 by the Emperor's agreement with the great *corps de l'état*, and ratify the *sénatus-consulte* of 20 April 1870.' The wording was cunning. To vote against the person of the Emperor it was also necessary to vote against the liberal reforms, while to vote in favour of the reforms was necessarily to vote in favour of the Emperor himself. The result was a massive 'yes' vote, 7.35 million to 1.5 million, with 1.9 million abstentions. The meaning of the plebiscite was hotly contested. Ollivier reckoned it a triumph for the liberal Empire. Authoritarian Bonapartists saw it as a vote of confidence in Napoleon himself, irrespective of constitutions. Republicans dismissed it as fraudulent, a victory achieved through manipulating the fears of the peasant masses. There was some justification for the republican viewpoint. Not only did the government run a strong 'yes' campaign, employing a familiar mix of stick and carrot, but, on the eve of the poll, Ollivier sensationally announced the arrest of all members of the International for their alleged involvement in a plot to assassinate the Emperor and to seize control of the state.

Nevertheless, there was no denying the scale of the government's victory, however achieved. The regime's share of the popular vote had increased by 3 million votes since the legislative elections of the previous year. After eighteen years in power, Napoleon III could still muster the support of 67.5 per cent of the electorate – a remarkable achievement, and testimony to his political skills. Only the larger cities remained hostile. In Paris it was the *quartiers populaires* (Belleville, the 11ᵉ, 12ᵉ, 18ᶜ *arrondissements*) which returned the greatest proportion of 'no' votes (76 per cent in Belleville). Saint-Etienne, with 77 per cent voting 'no', registered the highest level of opposition. Lyon also showed strong antipathy to the Empire (61 per cent), while Marseille remained the provincial capital of republicanism. In eastern France as a whole Bonapartist support had declined, but this was offset by gains in the north, north-east, lower Normandy, and many departments of the south-west and centre. Republicans could not but be disheartened. On 21 May, in a ceremony at the Louvre, Napoleon hailed the results as a triumph for the Empire over the forces of revolution.

After the plebiscite of 8 May 1870, the survival of the regime was not seriously in doubt. But a question mark did hang over the future of the liberal Empire. Despite Napoleon's promise to persist 'in the liberal line', the authoritarian Bonapartists were eager to be rid of Ollivier and to return to more congenially dictatorial ways. It was even whispered that the Emperor was plotting a second *coup d'état*: according to Haussmann, Napoleon spoke to him openly about it in June. The baron was probably deceiving himself. A coup was as unlikely as it was unnecessary. The original coup had been the source of many of Napoleon's troubles, and it is hard to imagine that he was keen to repeat the experiment. Whether he would have retained the Ollivier ministry for much longer is another matter. Ollivier was a brilliant orator but a poor parliamentarian, unable to conciliate the different factions in the Legislative Body. He had already lost Daru and Buffet, two centre-left members of his coalition who wanted nothing less than a return to the old parliamentary ways of the July Monarchy. With the Bonapartist right baying for his blood, it was not the minister, as he had fondly imagined, who was saving the Emperor, but rather Napoleon who, for a time, loyally upheld a cabinet which had already sorely tried his patience. How long he would have persisted can only be a matter for speculation. No servant was indispensable to Napoleon, who had no peer in the art of political intrigue and no scruple where the survival of the dynasty was concerned. The end of the Ollivier ministry would not have spelled the end of the regime. In 1870, only a catastrophe from outside the domestic political arena could have put the Empire itself in jeapardy. Unknown to Napoleon or anyone else, one was already brewing.

. . .

## NOTES AND REFERENCES

1. Quoted by Bury J P T 1964 *Napoleon III and the Second Empire.* English Universities Press, p. 108
2. 1985 'Crowning of edifice' in Echard W E (ed) *Historical Dictionary of the French Second Empire 1852–1870.* Greenwood Press
3. Ollivier E *L'Empire libéral: études, récits, souvenirs,* vol 14, pp. 538ff
4. McMillan J F 1981 *Housewife or Harlot: the Place of Women in French Society 1870–1940.* Harvester Press, p. 49; Rohr J 1967 *Victor Duruy, ministre de Napoléon III: essai sur la politique de l'instruction publique au temps de l'empire libéral*
5. Ollivier, vol 9, pp. 236–37
6. On Rochefort, see Williams R 1966 *Henri Rochefort, Prince of the Gutter Press.* Scribners
7. The words are J M Thompson's
8. Quoted by Zeldin T 1963 *Emile Ollivier and the Liberal Empire.* Clarendon Press, p. 122

9. Newton Lord 1913 *Lord Lyons: a Record of British Diplomacy*, 2 vols. Edward Arnold, vol 1, p. 242

10. Quoted by Corley T A B 1961 *Democratic Despot: a Life of Napoleon III*. Barrie & Rockliff, p. 311

11. Chapman J M and Chapman B 1957 *The Life and Times of Baron Haussmann*. Weidenfeld & Nicolson

12. Quoted by Ridley J 1979 *Napoleon III and Eugénie*. Constable, p. 552

13. The constitution is discussed by Zeldin 1963, ch. 10

*Chapter 9*

# A MODERN EMPEROR?

Any final verdict on Napoleon III must take into account his relationship with what many historians would regard as the most significant feature of the Second Empire: namely, the creation of a modern dynamic and expanding economy. Napoleon himself wished to be thought of as the emperor who brought prosperity to his people. Around 1868 he began to sketch out the plot of a novel whose central character was a Monsieur Benoît, a grocer who had emigrated from France to the United States in 1847 and who returns in the spring of 1868, to be astounded at the transformations which the Empire had wrought. Not only is he amazed by the crowds who make their way to the Hôtel de Ville to vote rather than to riot, but he also marvels at the ubiquitous evidence of material progress – the railways, the telegraph, the rebuilding of Paris. Benoît observes also that the cost of living has been lowered by the introduction of free trade, and that working people benefit from new welfare measures in addition to the right to strike.[1] Napoleon's novel was never written, but its projected themes suggest a fairly clear picture of how the Emperor wished to be remembered by posterity.

In recent years, a number of historians have been inclined to agree with the Emperor's assessment of his achievements. In place of the despot and bungling adventurer familiar in liberal, republican and socialist historiography, he emerges as a far-sighted technocrat and social reformer.[2] But is the latest 'reinvention' of Napoleon III any less of a distortion than earlier portrayals?

. . .

## 'SAINT-SIMON ON HORSEBACK'?

Even in the first half of the nineteenth century France was by no means as economically 'backward' as Anglo-Saxon economic historians once liked to think. Few experts now believe that the British model supplies the criteria by which French economic performance should be judged. Crude comparative figures for the output of coal, iron and cotton are not in themselves particularly informative. Recent quantitative work has established that, when considered on a per capita basis to allow for French demographic inferiority, economic growth in France was roughly comparable to that in Britain.[3] In any case, the use of national aggregates is questionable, given the tremendous sectoral and regional disparities to be found in France. Even agriculture, which continued to employ the majority of the population, had its dynamic sectors in the 1840s. French industry produced high-quality textiles, and transport improved dramatically with the construction of about 29,000 kilometres of road and about 3,000 kilometres of new canals between 1814 and 1846. Railways, too, had begun to make some impact by the end of the July Monarchy.

Nevertheless, the Second Empire must still be seen as a period of remarkable economic growth. The average rate of industrial expansion was 2 per cent a year. The building industry boomed. The railways entered their golden age. In 1851 there were 3,248 kilometres of track: by 1869, 16,465. The coal mines of the Nord responded vigorously to the insatiable demand for fuel in the iron and steel industry. The Paris Bourse became a leading international money market.

French banking underwent major developments, if not the revolution suggested by older work (more recent research suggests that the Parisian *haute banque* was not as conservative and averse to capital investment as used to be thought).[4] The Bank of France continued to play a leading role in the financing of industry but other institutions opened up to extend new credit facilities. In 1852 the Crédit Foncier was established to finance urban rebuilding projects. The same year the Crédit Mobilier was set up by the brothers Pereire as an investment bank to channel savings towards investment in industry. In 1863, Henri Germain founded what would become France's largest bank, the Crédit Lyonnais, while the following year a Rothschild-dominated consortium established the Société Générale. Both old and new banking institutions facilitated (and themselves profited by) economic growth, even if millions of francs remained unavailable for investment on account of the traditional peasant penchant for hoarding.

Urbanisation was another characteristic feature of the age. In 1851, only 5.4 per cent of the French lived in towns of more than 50,000: in 1866 the proportion had risen to nearly 11 per cent. Expansion was most evident in the larger towns, and above all in the capital, where the population grew from 1.2 million in 1846 to almost 2 million by 1870. Other signs of the times were the emergence of the large department store (the first, the *Bon Marché*, was founded by Aristide Boucicault in 1852, and was soon followed by *Le Louvre* and *Printemps*) and the great industrial exhibitions staged in Paris in 1855 and 1867. The first, opened by the Emperor while he was in the midst of waging the Crimean War, proved a huge success, attracting some five million visitors (Queen Victoria among them). The second was intended to bear witness to the inexorable march of technological progress during Napoleon's reign, and brought him some badly needed favourable publicity at a time when he was beset by diplomatic and domestic problems. Not a few of Europe's monarchs arrived to marvel at the wonders of French industry.

It would, of course, be absurd to credit Napoleon personally with responsibility for the generation of economic growth. He was more the beneficiary than the begetter of economic prosperity. What can legitimately be claimed on his behalf is that he recognised the key role which the state could play in economic affairs by itself encouraging expansion and by creating the conditions which favoured development. That is not to say, however, that Napoleon was literally a 'Saint-Simon on horseback', in the phrase of Sainte-Beuve. The influence of Saint-Simonian doctrine under the Second Empire was largely mythical, invented by propagandists at the time, and subsequently exaggerated by twentieth-century historians.[5] By 1852, the Saint-Simonian sect had long been disbanded, and in any case their ideas were never wholly original. Saint-Simonians were not alone in believing in the importance of building up a strong industrial base, improving communications and allotting the state a directing role in the management of the economy. Certainly, former Saint-Simonians such as Michel Chevalier and the Pereire brothers were involved in the economic achievements of the Second Empire, but it is not possible to demonstrate that Napoleon III himself was directly influenced by Saint-Simonian thought.

Probably the most important contribution which Napoleon made personally to economic expansion was to provide the political stability which encouraged 'confidence' in the business community and to create a climate favourable to the expansion of capitalism. The readiness on the part of small savers to invest in the new banks, railways and the great public works programmes of the Second Empire testifies to the trust which the regime inspired. Napoleon also countenanced the new methods of borrowing and of deficit finance pioneered by the likes of the Pereires and Haussmann. Moreover, by raising vast loans, especially in wartime, directly by public subscription, the Second Empire was able to present itself as a promoter of popular capitalism. It claimed to be sustained by the 'universal suffrage of capital', since by 1868 there were some 672,000 subscribers to loans.[6] On the other hand, it should be noted that under the Empire the state itself did not finance public works through the budget, devoting less expenditure to them in the period 1852–59 than had the July Monarchy in the 1840s. The Empire's preference was to stimulate and to support private enterprise, and here it can claim credit for having introduced legislation to deregulate joint-stock companies and industry, and for having established closer links between industry and the state.

One area where the personal intervention of the Emperor himself was crucial was in the rebuilding of Paris. In June 1853 Napoleon appointed Georges Haussmann prefect of the Seine, and thereafter supported his grandiose plans and unorthodox financial methods in the face of strong opposition from many quarters, including from several leading ministers. Together, Napoleon and Haussmann created the modern city of Paris to which tourists still delight to flock in the late twentieth century. Progress had its price, of course – much of the medieval city was ruthlessly destroyed and workers were expelled from the centre to new slums on the periphery – but the gains were undeniable. In 1859, the boundaries of the city were extended to increase the number of administrative districts (*arrondissements*) from twelve to twenty. The infrastructure was completely overhauled by the building of new sewage, drainage and water supply systems. The centre was transformed by the building of new streets, breath-taking boulevards, beautiful parks and handsome buildings. Five new bridges were constructed over the Seine, and six others rebuilt. New markets were erected, most strikingly the Halles Centrales (now themselves a victim of so-called urban renewal). The rebuilding also encompassed new railway stations, theatres (of which the most famous was Garnier's Opéra), churches, schools, town halls and the reading room of the Bibliothèque Nationale, as well as elegant apartment blocks. While it is true that drastic transformations would have had to take place in the city's physiognomy in any event in order to cope with the demographic and public health problems posed by its continuing expansion, the fact remains that the final outcome was a monument to the preoccupations – strategic and political as well as aesthetic – of Napoleon and Haussmann.

The other area where the hand of the Emperor was much in evidence was in the push to liberalise trade, epitomised in the Free Trade Treaty signed with Britain in January 1860. Most French manufacturers, particularly those in the textiles and metallurgical industries, were strongly committed to protectionism, but from the outset Napoleon III's government began to lower tariff duties (for instance, on iron, steel and coal) with a view to expanding trade and raising the living standards of the poorest classes. In the mid-1850s, there were plans to extend the policy to all commodities, but the pressure brought to bear by outraged industrialists forced the government to desist. The treaty of 1860 was therefore prepared in the utmost secrecy, without discussion in the Council of Ministers, let alone in the Legislative Body. The timing was affected by political as well as economic considerations, for in late 1859 Napoleon was as anxious to repair relations with Britain after the Italian war as to reinvigorate the economy after the slump of 1857.

The moving spirit in France was Michel Chevalier, one of the Emperor's top economic advisers and a friend of Richard Cobden, the prominent British free trader. Chevalier and Cobden were the principal negotiators of the treaty which was signed on 22 January, and which provided for massive reductions in French duties levied on British goods alongside free entry of French goods, except wines and spirits, into the British market. The treaty also served as a model for further bilateral deals which France concluded with other European countries.

Whether its impact was as sweepingly beneficial as apologists for free trade have claimed may be doubted, while its allegedly harmful effects were similarly exaggerated by the protectionist lobby. The latest thinking of economic historians is that probably the treaty did little to alter long-term patterns of trade.[7] Nevertheless, the Emperor must be credited with a bold step in the interests of international trade, especially when his initiative was bound to provoke hostile reactions among sections of the French bourgeoisie which, hitherto, had been strong supporters of the regime of 2 December.

A greater novelist than Napoleon III, Zola, was as impressed as Monsieur Benoît at the emergence of a new France characterised by department stores, railways, modern industry and the omnipotence of money. Yet, great as the economic changes effected under the Second Empire were, they tell only part of the story. If growth was extremely rapid between 1852 and 1857, it slowed down after 1860. Economic crises did not disappear. Those of 1857 and 1866–67 were severe, if temporary, setbacks. The collapse of the Crédit Mobilier in 1867 had symbolic, as well as financial, implications: some took the crash of the Pereire financial empire to be a harbinger of the downfall of the regime itself. Moreover, as some sectors prospered, others declined. Certain areas experienced de-industrialisation: the south-east, for instance, where the textile industries declined, and the south-west, where the woollen industry succumbed to competition from the more technically advanced producers from the north who now had access to a national market via the railway network.

Archaic structures still characterised much of French agriculture. The parcellisation of the land increased between 1852 and the end of the Empire (holdings of below 10 hectares constituted 68 per cent of agricultural establishments in 1852 and 85 per cent in 1882). The demographic trend was also worryingly downward, as the population grew from 35.8 million in 1851 to only 36.1 million in 1872. Even if the latter figure is exacerbated by the loss of Alsace-Lorraine, the birth-rate of 1866–69 was 26.1, more or less what it had been right through the Second Empire, but down substantially on the figure of 28.1 for the period 1841–45. Overall, the performance of the regime in the economic sphere corresponded with its record in other spheres: which is to say, it was mixed.

. . .

## SOCIAL POLICY

Napoleon's hope was that economic modernisation would serve to eliminate the strife which had divided the French since the time of the Revolution. Prosperity would be the harbinger of social peace. Bonapartist propaganda continually stressed that the Emperor was the friend of the worker. As Napoleon told a workers' delegation at the outset of the reign, 'Those who work and those who suffer can count on me.'[8]

It would be unfair to suggest that the Emperor's efforts on behalf of the labouring poor were motivated simply by propaganda considerations rather than genuine concern. True, he did not depart from the belief current under the July Monarchy that the most effective remedy for poverty was private charity: hence the channelling of government funds into relief works and programmes of public works. The lavishness of the imperial couple's own donations to charity was legendary, and Napoleon saw to it that among those to be aided were the unemployed and the urban poor as well as the victims of natural disasters. Charities were founded to provide homes for convalescent workers, apprenticeships for orphans, nurseries for working mothers. Encouragement was also given to workers' mutual aid societies, low-cost housing projects, public baths and public assistance generally.

Napoleon, however, was responsible for new initiatives which were meant to identify the regime's sympathies with working people more overtly. The most important was the law of 25 May 1864 (piloted through the Legislative Body by Emile Ollivier) which legalised strikes (but not trade unions). It followed a plea from a workers' delegation, headed by the Proudhonist bronze-worker Tolain, which, with the Emperor's blessing, had attended the London Exhibition of 1862, and the Emperor's personal intervention in the printers' strikes of 1863 to quash the sentences passed against its leaders. Workers were quick to avail themselves of their new freedom under the law of 1864 and, in the wake of strike movements in that year and in 1865 and 1867, the regime announced its *de facto* recognition of workers' associations. Napoleon made substantial financial contributions to a fund to develop workers' cooperatives and he also changed the law in 1868 to remove the stipulation in the Civil Code that, in an industrial dispute, an employer's word should always be accepted before that of a worker. He further announced his intention of bringing in old-age pensions for workers and, after his fall, was to lament that other reforms designed to benefit the working classes had been blocked by the Council of State. It was because he saw it as an ally against the conservative elites that he initially looked with favour on the founding of the Working Men's International in 1864.

Yet neither the regime's 'state socialism' nor the generalisation of prosperity won the majority of workers over to Bonapartism. As has already been shown, it was the populations of the larger cities who remained the most intransigent opponents of the Second Empire. For, if living standards rose (as may be seen, for instance, in the greater consumption of food and drink) and if wages also began to rise, so, too, did prices. The economic boom created huge class differentials between the rich and the urban poor, some of whom, like the textile workers of Lille or the hideously exploited female domestic workers of the Parisian clothing industry, frequently lived in squalor. As the episode of the Paris Commune of 1871 would reveal, Parisian workers also bitterly resented *haussmannisation*, which drove them out to exile in the *banlieue*. The Second Empire was a crucial period in the development of a sense of militancy and class consciousness on the part of workers in France, and its final years witnessed a renewed outbreak of serious industrial unrest.[9] In the Lyon region in 1869–70, a strike wave, coordinated by members of the International, brought out an impressive range of workers who included miners, weavers, building workers and textile workers. In Alsace in July 1870 15,000 workers went on strike. It has been claimed that most of these strikes were not political, and that they represented, rather, a protest against the rising cost of living. But whether or not workers sided with bourgeois republican critics of the regime, their action exposes the hollowness of the Empire's claims to have eliminated class antagonisms and to have instituted a new era of stability through the spread of prosperity and technocratic progress.

. . .

## COLONIAL EXPANSION

It was Napoleon's preoccupation with economic prosperity as much as the thirst for *grandeur* and military glory which led him to pursue a policy of colonial expansion. As a prisoner at Ham, he had already turned his mind to colonial questions, notably that of the sugar trade with the West Indies, though at that time his sympathies were with domestic cultivators of sugar-beet against the colonial producers.[10] As in the matter of free trade, however, Napoleon came to see the colonial issue in a different light once he had come to power.

His inheritance consisted largely of the scattered left-overs of the French empire of the *ancien régime*: Martinique and Guadeloupe in the West Indies; a forgotten part of Guiana; the fishing ports of St Pierre and Miquelon, off Newfoundland; a few footholds in West Africa; Bourbon Island (Réunion) and its neighbours in the Indian Ocean; and some trading posts in the Indian sub-continent. The most notable addition to these had been Algeria, the conquest of which had begun under the Restored Bourbons and had continued under the July Monarchy, despite Louis Philippe's reservations about the enterprise. The July Monarchy had also added other islands in the Indian and Pacific oceans, but it could hardly be said that, upon his access to power, Napoleon's imperial inheritance was impressive.

His first thought was to reorganise the relationship between the colonies and the mother country. In May 1854, by *senatus-consultum*, he divided them into two categories, the 'great colonies', consisting of Réunion and the Antilles, to be regulated by *senatus-consultum*, and the rest, which were placed under the direct rule of the Emperor's government via the Ministry of Marine (after 1860, the Ministry of Marine and the Colonies). Over the course of the reign, Napoleon worked to introduce free-trade policies in the colonies, abandoning the mercantilist doctrines which had subordinated their trade to the interests of the mother country. Even before becoming Emperor, in 1851, he allowed a reduction in the tariff on colonial sugar, despite his earlier support for protectionism. In the colonial Empire, as in his dealings with Britain, Napoleon showed himself to be a 'modern' and a 'liberal' in so far as he favoured the creation of a world market.

Algeria became the chief focus of Napoleon's plans for economic expansion outside France. At Ham, his reading had included the Saint-Simonian Enfantin's *La colonisation de l'Algérie*, which envisaged Algeria as the meeting-ground of East and West, though, as Emperor, it seems most likely that, in the first instance, his concern with the colony was prompted by the immediate problem of 'pacification' – a euphemism for the bloody repression carried out by the French military, notably by Marshal Bugeaud between 1841 and 1847. After the *coup d'état*, General Randon was appointed as governor-general, and by 1858, when he relinquished office, native resistance, even that of the fierce Berbers, had been crushed, though the history of French Algeria would long continue to be punctuated by serious rebellions and uprisings. Napoleon appreciated that colonisation and economic development were required to consolidate the position established by the military. In conformity with Saint-Simonian doctrine, and to underline the special importance he attached to Algeria, he replaced military with civilian authority, creating a Ministry of Algeria and the Colonies in 1858, with his cousin Prince Napoleon at its head. Plon-Plon was convinced that the colony could best be run from Paris, and never set foot in it during his tenure of the ministry. His policy was to push ahead with 'assimilation', by which Algeria was ruled as far as was possible like any other department of France. The settlers were delighted, both at the end of military rule and at the extension of their privileges. The losers were the indigenous population, driven from their lands to make way for the settlers and confined to *cantonnements*, designated areas of the interior where they were subjected to 'Frenchification'. When Prince Napoleon resigned after only ten months in office, his successor, the marquis de Chasseloup-Laubat, continued his policies, making further concessions to the Europeans for railway development and initiating a large-scale public works programme.

The brief experiment in civilian government, however, was terminated by the Emperor after he visited the colony in person in the summer of 1860. Military rule was restored under the brutal General Pélissier as governor-general. Pélissier identified strongly with the settlers, but Napoleon had been moved by the plight of the natives and by the arguments of Arabophile army officers (among them the Saint-Simonian Ishmail Urbain) who pointed out that 'assimilation' and *cantonnement* were a recipe for endemic rebellion. Their solution was to establish an Arab Kingdom, in which the army would assume a paternalistic and humanitarian role. Napoleon tried to make their policy his own, telling Pélissier in a letter of 1 November 1861 that he should avoid reducing the native Algerians to a state comparable to that of the American Indians. After conversations with native

Arab chiefs, invited by the Emperor to Compiègne in 1862, and consultations with influential politicians such as Baron Jérôme David, Napoleon published an open letter to Pélissier in the *Moniteur* of 6 February 1863 affirming his intention to be 'Emperor of the Arabs' and protector of their rights. *Cantonnement* was stopped, and a *senatus-consultum* of April 1863 confirmed natives in their rights to their lands.

Another outbreak of native protest in 1864 merely confirmed the Emperor in his view that the tribes had to be treated with respect by the *colons*. Once order had been restored, he made a second trip to Algeria in May 1865 and on his return sent a lengthy analysis of the situation to the new governor-general, Marshal MacMahon. Criticising previous policies in the colony, he insisted that it should be treated as 'at the same time an Arab Kingdom, a European colony, and a French military establishment'. Neither the Marshal nor the settlers were impressed by the Emperor's pleas for fair play for the natives. Nor was the metropolitan of Algiers, Archbishop Lavigerie, content to leave the Muslims in peace, when they could be subjected to proselytising which might result in the resurrection of the African Church of St Augustine. The colonial lobby continued to agitate for the restoration of civilian rule, and carried the day eventually in the Legislative Body in 1870 – a development which helped to precipitate yet another major uprising on the part of the Arabs in 1871.

It can certainly be argued that Napoleon III took a more enlightened view of Algerian colonisation than was to be found among either the settlers or the military. In that respect, perhaps, his policy can be regarded as 'modern' and in tune with the thinking not only of the Saint-Simonians but also of liberals like Prévost-Paradol, who in his influential book *La Nouvelle France* (1868) identified a thriving Algeria as an important guarantor of France's vigour as a great power. The *senatus-consultum* of July 1865, which facilitated the naturalisation of all inhabitants of Algeria, was a practical gesture towards the creation of such a larger France. What Napoleon never questioned, however, was the rightness of the French presence in the first place. From a post-colonial perspective, he can hardly be called a true modern. In so far as the Second Empire consolidated the conquest, it stored up trouble not only in the short term but also for the next century. Algeria was less an advertisement for the Emperor's statecraft than for his idealism and good intentions – both of which were frequently at odds with the moral and material interests of France.

Algeria was a key element in Napoleon III's designs to bring the Mediterranean under French domination, but not necessarily the first step towards the creation of a larger North African Empire. Thus, he made no attempt to take over neighbouring Morocco or Tunis. Rather, he looked towards the eastern end of the Mediterranean in the hope of realising another 'Napoleonic idea' – namely, to link the Mediterranean with the Red Sea by means of a canal built at Suez. The project had fascinated the Emperor's uncle and was then taken up in earnest by Saint-Simonian visionaries such as Enfantin and Chevalier, who dreamed of marrying East and West, but it was Ferdinand de Lesseps who, having first become enthusiastic about the idea while serving with the French consulate in Cairo in 1832, was destined to bring it to fulfilment. Even so, it was over twenty years later before he set up his international company to finance the scheme in 1854 and five years after that before work actually began.

Apart from the formidable technical difficulties involved, the main obstacles encountered by de Lesseps were political. Palmerston headed a noisy anti-canal lobby in Britain, and the Sultan of Turkey, overlord of Egypt, was likewise hostile. Here the engineer was lucky in being able to gain the ear of Napoleon III, partly because of his being a cousin of the Empress, but more because Napoleon saw how the project would benefit international trade in general and French interests in particular. (He was, after all, the author of the earlier Nicaraguan Canal scheme.) Napoleon personally acquired shares in the Suez Canal Company, and, when it became necessary to force the hand of the Porte to allow the work to continue, he did not shrink from doing so in 1865. The extraordinary feat of engineering was completed in 1869, and at the spectacular opening ceremony of 17 November, the Empress Eugenie was present in the imperial yacht *l'Aigle* at the head of some forty ships which sailed through the canal. For once, Napoleon III's enterprise and imagination brought him glory and material rewards.

Napoleon's influence at the eastern end of the Mediterranean was reinforced by continuing French involvement in the affairs of the Near East. When in 1860 the Muslim Druses of the Lebanon began to massacre Maronite Christians and were then emulated by their co-religionists in Syria, Napoleon was ready to intervene on behalf of the victims. French troops were dispatched to Beirut, with international approval, though Napoleon was told that the French presence was to be for a limited period only. Nevertheless, the show of force confirmed France's interest in the area – an interest which was as much economic as religious, since the region was an important supplier of raw silk for the French market. After the withdrawal of French troops, Napoleon was able to press successfully for the establishment of an autonomous Lebanon ruled by a Christian governor.

The Far East, too, figured in Napoleon's global vision. As in the Near East, religion provided the pretext for intervention, since Catholic missionaries suffered persecution both in China and in Indo-China, and Napoleon was all the more willing to help them because of criticism from the ranks of French Catholics angered by his Italian policy. Economic considerations, however, were again not foreign to his actions. Since the Treaty of Nanking of 1842, which had ended the first 'Opium' war in China, French merchants had established themselves in some of the principal cities on the Chinese mainland. It was to consolidate and extend their privileges (as well as to curry favour with Britain) that Napoleon sent a French force along with the British in 1856. Together they bombarded Canton, and in 1860 marched on Peking, where they sacked the fabulous 'Summer Palace' of the Chinese emperor. In its barbarity and indifference to the rights of indigenous peoples, the Chinese expedition may be regarded as all too 'modern'. As Victor Hugo wrote at the time, it was an act of international banditry and wanton destruction.[11]

In Indo-China, the appeals of missionaries in the face of ferocious persecution persuaded Napoleon to send a French fleet in 1857. The French joined forces with a Spanish expedition, and Saigon was taken easily enough, but the ruler of Annam, Tu-Duc, put up strong resistance, obliging the French to send reinforcements to their disease-ravaged troops. By 1865, however, they had established their authority in Cochin-China and compelled the Annamese emperor to permit Catholics to practise their religion openly. The King of Cambodia also agreed to the establishment of a French protectorate. Napoleon was at first greatly excited by the commercial prospects opened up in the fabulous Orient by these conquests, but, as he plunged deeper into the mire of the Mexican adventure, he contemplated renouncing them. He was dissuaded by Chasseloup-Laubat, his Minister of Marine and the Colonies, and the French maintained their presence in the area. The work of extending the French Empire in Indo-China belonged to the future, but the basis of French rule had certainly been laid by the end of Napoleon III's reign. France was to retain its colony of Indo-China until 1954, but once again it would be difficult to support the view that the extension of the French *imperium* was an unqualified good.

There were other colonial acquisitions. In 1853, the French occupied New Caledonia in the Pacific and turned it into a penal colony. Napoleon also approved the forward policy of General Faidherbe, appointed Governor-General of Sénégal in 1854, who over the course of the next ten years pushed inland to lay the basis of the colony of French West Africa, likewise destined to last until the second half of the twentieth century. Having built the port of Dakar and established trading contacts with the Sudan, Faidherbe succeeded in developing an export industry of the region's raw materials. Further to the south, the French also penetrated the Guinean and Ivory coasts.

Taken together, Napoleon III's colonial exploits add up to a considerable, if not necessarily premeditated or closely co-ordinated, effort to establish France as not just a European but a world power. His desire to build up the French navy, viewed with alarm in London, can be construed in the same light. His ambitions may have been 'modern', but (saving the Suez Canal) his enterprises cannot be deemed to have been wise. Most of the time, he stored up trouble either for himself or for future generations. Nowhere was his ill-judgement more evident than in the Mexican adventure. Rouher styled this 'the great idea of the reign', but it ended in tragedy and humiliation.

. . .

## MEXICO

Precisely why Napoleon should have become embroiled in the affairs of Central America is still a matter of debate. Probably, as so often, his motives were mixed. An interest in the gener-ation of wealth through technological innovation was certainly one factor. Since his time in prison at Ham, he had thought of Mexico as a point where East and West might be linked to form the pivot of a vast commercial empire. Mexico had the further advantage that its silver deposits could be used to stabilise the French currency. Yet another consideration was that Napoleon had become sensitive to the growing power of the United States, and was keen to build up a countervailing force to the south. A strong Mexico, either alone or as part of a larger Central American state, could check, if not reverse, the advances already made by the United States at the expense of Mexico. Then again, quite apart from its economic attractions, Mexico seemed to offer a fresh field for the extension of Napoleon's diplomatic initiatives in Europe. Not only would a stake in a Latin-American empire enhance his prestige at home, but, in addition, it might allow him to repair the damage to relations with Austria caused by his Italian policies through the creation of a Franco-Austrian imperial partnership in the New World.

The 'great idea' was to establish the Austrian Archduke Maximilian, brother of the Emperor Francis Joseph, as Emperor of Mexico. It matured slowly, against a background of troubled relations between France and Mexico. Since 1821, when Mexico had acquired independence from Spain, the country had been wracked by civil strife and subjected to acute political instability. In consequence, French traders, second in number to the Spaniards, frequently found themselves expropriated and victimised by successive Mexican governments. Even the pacifically inclined Louis Philippe had been moved to send troops to Veracruz in 1838 in an attempt to obtain redress. The situation continued to deteriorate, however, and the victory in 1857 of the 'liberal' and violently anticlerical faction headed by Juarez in the civil war of the 1850s seemed to bode ill for both the French and the Church, all the more so since Juarez favoured closer relations with the United States. Napoleon's displeasure at this outcome was compounded by his belief that, because of their race and temperament, the 'Latins' of South America required the firm smack of monarchical rather than republican rule. He therefore listened with interest to Mexican expatriates in Paris who told him that, with foreign help, the strongly entrenched monarchical party in Mexico could yet carry the day.

Yet, preoccupied with events in Europe and wary of provoking the United States by violating the 'Monroe Doctrine', Napoleon was in no hurry to act, despite the entreaties of Eugénie, who had been completely won over by Hidalgo, the chief spokesman for the Mexican exiles, and the machinations of Saligny, the French representative in Mexico, who wanted

French intervention for his own sordid financial reasons. It was the outbreak of the American Civil War in 1861 which persuaded Napoleon that action might be possible while the United States could offer no effective opposition.

The pretext was provided by Juarez's suspension of payments to all foreign creditors in July 1861. Representatives of France, Spain and Britain met in London at the end of October and agreed on joint action to compel the Mexicans to honour their debts. That Napoleon envisaged more than a mere debt-collecting exercise, however, is evident from the negotiations he entered into at roughly the same time with Archduke Maximilian in connection with effecting a monarchical restoration in Mexico. News of this plan alienated Britain and Spain, who withdrew their troops from the expeditionary force which had been sent to Veracruz in December 1861, leaving the French to face the Mexicans alone, and to suffer a defeat at Puebla in May 1862. They soon discovered that the enthusiasm for monarchy depicted by the Mexican exiles in Paris was virtually non-existent. It required considerable reinforcements and another year of fighting before French troops were in a position to enter Mexico City and to set up a provisional government, which proceeded to offer the throne to Maximilian.

He accepted, and arrived in the country with his young wife Charlotte, daughter of King Leopold of the Belgians, in 1864, having first signed the convention of Miromar (10 April 1864) with Napoleon III, whereby he got the French Emperor to promise his military support for another three years. But Napoleon drove a hard bargain. He already entertained misgivings about the affair, not least because of its unpopularity in France, and insisted that the financial costs of the occupation be transferred to Mexico rather than France. He also carefully refrained from promising to defend the new Mexican regime indefinitely, or in any conflict which might ensue with the United States. His caution in the latter regard was well founded, when in December 1865 the North finally triumphed over the South in the American Civil War, and the United States government immediately made clear both its support for Juarez and its intention of removing European influence from the Americas in conformity with the Monroe Doctrine. At a time when Napoleon was perturbed by the prospect of a war with Prussia, he could ill afford a conflict with the United States, or even to keep 30,000–40,000 troops tied down in Mexico.

Despite desperate entreaties from the Empress Charlotte, who returned to Europe in July 1866 to beg Napoleon not to abandon her husband, he began to pull out, leaving Maximilian at the mercy of Juarez. In May 1867 he was betrayed and taken prisoner, and on 19 June executed before a firing squad. His wife, meantime, had gone out of her mind, and died, still insane, in 1927. The 'great idea' ended both in personal tragedy and in humiliation for Napoleon III. Never popular with the French public, it greatly exacerbated the difficulties which Napoleon was already experiencing in the aftermath of Sadowa, and cast a dark shadow over the last years of the reign.

. . . .

## NOTES AND REFERENCES

1. *Papiers et correspondance de la famille impériale*, vol 1, p. 218
2. See in particular Blanchard M 1950 *Le Second Empire*; Duveau G 1957 'Qui est cet homme?', *Miroir de l'Histoire* 8, pp. 231–36: Corley T A B 1961, *Democratic Despot: a Life of Napoleon III*. Barrie & Rockliff
3. Lévy-Leboyer M 1968 'Les processus d'industrialisation: le cas de l'Angleterre et de la France', *Revue Historique* 239, pp. 281–98
4. Plessis A 1982 *La Banque de France et ses deux cents actionnaires sous le Second Empire*. Droz; 1984 *Régents et gouverneurs de la Banque de France sous le Second Empire*. Droz
5. On this see 1985 'Saint-Simonianism' in Echard W E (ed) in *Historical Dictionary of the French Second Empire 1852–1870*. Greenwood Press
6. Plessis A 1985 *Rise and Fall of the Second Empire 1852–1871*. Cambridge University Press, p. 64
7. Ratcliffe B M 1875 'Napoleon III and the Anglo-French Commercial Treaty of 1860: a Reconsideration', in Ratcliffe B M (ed) *Great Britain and Her World 1750–1914*. Manchester University Press
8. Kulstein D 1969 *Napoleon III and the Working Class: a Study of Government Propaganda under the Second Empire*. California State Colleges
9. See L'Huillier F L 1957 *La Lutte Ouvrière à la fin du Second Empire*
10. Bonaparte L N 1842 *Analyse de la question des sucres*
11. Quoted by Ridley J *Napoleon III and Eugénie*, p. 472

# Chapter 10

# FALL FROM POWER

In the early summer of 1870, liberalisation appeared to have given the Second Empire a new lease of life. The liberal ministry had weathered the storms of its first months in office and had embarked on a broad programme of reform. On 30 June, Ollivier told the Legislative Body that the plebiscite of May ought to be regarded as a 'French Sadowa'. He added: 'at no epoch was the peace of Europe more assured'.[1]

The pacific intentions of the liberal ministers were not in doubt. In Count Napoleon Daru, formerly one of the deputies of the Second Republic who had tried to organise resistance to the *coup d'état* in 1851, Ollivier had a foreign minister who shared his own commitment to peace and arms reduction. Despite Prussian coolness to their overtures, they went ahead with a reduction of the French contingent from 100,000 to 90,000 as a gesture of good will. A liberal Catholic and neo-Gallican, Daru had reservations about the portending declaration of papal infallibility at the Vatican Council convoked by Pius IX, but Ollivier convinced Napoleon III that this was a purely ecclesiastical matter where French governmental intervention was inappropriate. As far as the German question was concerned, Ollivier was prepared to accept the unification of northern and southern Germany should the people themselves demand it. On the other hand, he was no pacifist, indifferent to the claims of French grandeur: rather the opposite. Under no circumstances was he prepared to accept a slight to French honour, especially from Prussia. As he put it to the British ambassador, '*un échec, c'est la guerre*'.[2] Indeed, precisely because his ministry, unlike its predecessors, was accountable to parliament, he considered it less able to tolerate any affront to national pride. Ollivier had shown firmness in dealing with the challenge of the left. He meant to be equally tough with truculent foreigners. That explains why, two days after his 'French Sadowa' speech, he reacted with indignation to the news that a Hohenzollern prince had been offered and had accepted the vacant throne of Spain.

. . .

## THE HOHENZOLLERN CRISIS

Prince Leopold of Hohenzollern-Sigmaringen was a distant relative of King William of Prussia and a slightly less distant one of Napoleon III. In upbringing, however, he was thoroughly Prussian, and the idea that he should become King of Spain in the place of the deposed Isabella II conjured up French fears of 'encirclement' by Prussia as well as adding yet another item to the long list of French grievances which had been accumulating against that power since 1866. According to the diplomatic conventions of the time the French were justified in taking an active interest in what, at one level, could be regarded as a purely internal Spanish matter: it involved the balance of power. At the earliest rumours of a Hohenzollern candidacy the French government had not been slow to reveal its concern. In March 1869, Benedetti was told that their suspicions were groundless. When the rumours persisted, he saw Bismarck in May, only to receive another denial. Rightly, the ambassador expressed scepticism about the Prussian reply (Bismarck had in fact been responsible for leaking the secret negotiations between the Spaniards and Leopold to the press). The candidate himself was fearful of provoking France. His first instincts were to decline the offer. King William was likewise reticent. Bismarck, however, came to relish the prospect of 'complications' – the kind of European crisis which might advance his own schemes for the unification of non-Austrian Germany and permit him to overcome the considerable domestic problems which he faced (notably the determined opposition of Catholic particularists to his expansionist designs).

Bismarck never doubted that the French response to the prospect of a Hohenzollern on the throne of Spain would be vigorous. Napoleon III's preference was for a regency until Alfonso, Isabella's son, could assume the throne. He actively lobbied against the candidatures of Ferdinand of Portugal and of the duc de Montpensier, youngest son of Louis Philippe. His fear was that no foreign prince would be able to establish his authority in Spain. Should a Hohenzollern prince be over-thrown, Prussia might be tempted to go to his assistance, confronting France with a situation reminiscent of the threat from Habsburg power in the sixteenth century. In any case, another Prussian diplomatic success at the expense of France was not to be tolerated. Nevertheless, he could see how Bismarck's manoeuvres might ultimately be turned to France's advantage. If the German Chancellor could be unmasked for the troublemaker he was, France might be able to inflict a diplomatic humiliation on Prussia. Sadowa would be avenged and Napoleon's critics silenced. Hence, instead of putting pressure on Spain to drop the Hohenzollern candidacy, Napoleon allowed the affair to build up to the point where France could legitimately intervene to take a hardline stance. It was a high-risk policy. It *almost* worked – but in the end it went disastrously wrong.

Matters came to a head on 2 July 1870, when word leaked to Paris that Leopold had finally given his consent to the Spaniards. Napoleon was told officially on 3 July by Gramont, the new Foreign Minister. (He had replaced Daru following the latter's resignation over the constitutional issue of the Emperor's refusal to seek parliamentary approval for the holding of the referendum.) Antoine, duc de Gramont, was a career diplomat who had served for eight years at the court of Vienna and was notorious for his pro-Austrian and anti-Prussian sentiments. Neither he nor Napoleon necessarily wanted war with Prussia, but they were ready to seize on an issue which might afford them the long-sought diplomatic coup. For Napoleon the crisis came at a bad time. On the same day that he received the news of the Hohenzollern candidacy, a leading specialist diagnosed the need for further exploration of his bladder problem.[3] Whether or not Napoleon received a full account of the diagnosis is uncertain, but he knew that he was a sick man. On the other hand, his illness was not such that he easily fell prey to the war party in his entourage, which was headed by the Empress. The Emperor was still in charge of foreign policy, all the more so given the inexperience of Gramont and Ollivier. It may be, however, that he felt the need for his diplomatic triumph sooner rather than later.

The ambassadors at Berlin and Madrid were immediately instructed to make representations against the nomination of Leopold. On 4 July, Ollivier, eager not to be outdone in patriotism by his enemies on the Bonapartist right, joined Gramont in denouncing the candidature to Werther, the Prussian ambassador in Paris. Together, they urged him to prevail on his king to make Leopold desist. A statement from a spokesman in Berlin to the effect that, as far as the Prussian government was concerned, the affair did not exist, merely reinforced French determination to have satisfaction. Napoleon had Gramont draft a statement for parliament, which was unanimously approved by the council when it met on the morning of 6 July. (There is no truth to the story that Napoleon wanted a less harshly worded text.)[4] In the afternoon Gramont read his declaration to the deputies, which concluded with an unmistakable threat. Should neither Spain nor Prussia back down, he promised, 'we shall know how to discharge our duty without faltering or weakness'. To a deputy who exclaimed, 'But this is war! This is a challenge that you are hurling at Prussia!', Gramont replied: 'It is peace if that is possible, it is war if that is inevitable.'[5]

Napoleon and his ministers were playing a very dangerous game. For people who wanted to avoid war they were making extremely bellicose noises. At the council meeting on the morning of 6 July the military and diplomatic situations had also been discussed. Marshal Leboeuf, Minister of War, gave assurances that the army was ready, and argued for war before Prussia was better prepared. Napoleon himself ended the debate as to whether Austria or Russia would make the better ally (Gramont favoured the former and Ollivier the latter) by hinting that both Austria and Italy were likely to side with France in a contest with Prussia. Napoleon also told Gramont to contact the Russian foreign minister to inform him that, if Prussia insisted on maintaining the Hohenzollern candidature, 'it will be war'.[6] Benedetti was ordered to break off his vacation and make for Bad Ems to be able to speak face to face with King William in order to determine whether he had authorised the candidature. Repeated messages from Paris stressed the urgency of his mission. One dated 10 July, from Gramont, read: 'If the king won't advise the prince of Hohenzollern to renounce, well, it's immediate war and in a few days we'll be on the Rhine.'[7] Napoleon himself, after private consultations with Leboeuf, ordered the commencement of military preparations, sending word to Marshal MacMahon in Algeria to start embarking his troops as soon as possible. On 10 July he broached the subject of Italian aid with Ambassador Nigra, offering in exchange the withdrawal of French troops from Civita Vecchia.

Yet, despite all the sabre-rattling, Napoleon still hoped to resolve the situation without war. Unknown to his ministers, he had been manoeuvring behind their backs to find a peaceful outcome. On 5 July he asked Baron Alfons Rothschild to use his influence with Gladstone to try to convince the British statesman of the need to make Leopold stand down. Likewise, he wrote to the King of Belgium requesting that he in turn write personally to Leopold. Most effectively, he persuaded Olozaga, the Spanish ambassador in Paris, to appeal to Leopold to withdraw. The combination of carrot and stick had their effect. While (like most of the leading *dramatis personae*) Leopold too was away on vacation, reputedly in the Alps, his father Karl Anton, much troubled by the upheaval to which his son's acceptance of the throne of Spain had given rise, took it upon himself to renounce the Hohenzollern candidature on his son's behalf. On 12 July news of his decision reached Paris. Even Thiers, the consistently bitter critic of Prussian aggrandisement, conceded that 'Sadowa is almost avenged'. The veteran Guizot spoke of 'the finest diplomatic victory I have ever seen'. Shrewd foreign observers such as Lord Lyons and Nigra also acknowledged a French victory and counselled Gramont not to look for more.[8] The crisis seemed to be over.

Napoleon himself at first considered the matter closed. As he told Nigra, not without more than a hint of regret, the renunciation meant peace, 'at least for the moment', even though the public would have preferred war.[9] A conversation with Gramont changed his mind. The Foreign Minister argued that Karl Anton's statement was not in itself sufficient to conclude the incident. What was required was nothing less than a guarantee that the candidature would never be renewed. After all, the renunciation had not even come from the candidate himself but from his father – 'le père Antoine', as the deputies of the right called him derisorily. How could one be sure that Leopold himself, supposedly enjoying the pleasures of the Alps, was not in fact on his way to Spain? Had not his brother defied his sovereign and taken himself off to be crowned King of Romania in 1866? More crucially, Gramont had little difficulty in persuading Napoleon to believe that, whatever the diplomats thought, public opinion in France expected more than this 'Sadowa of the salons'. Instead of trying to calm tempers, as

Ollivier would have preferred, Napoleon and Gramont stepped up their pressure on Prussia in conformity with the wilder xenophobic utterances from the streets. Without consulting Ollivier, the Emperor and his Foreign Minister drew up new instructions for Benedetti to seek reassurances from the Prussian king that he would veto any future attempt to put a Hohenzollern on the throne of Spain. It was a fatal *démarche*, in all probability anticipated by Bismarck.[10] Only marginally less maladroit was the suggestion put to the Prussian ambassador by Gramont and Ollivier that he invite his sovereign to write what would have been in effect a letter of apology to France. These moves led inexorably to defeat being snatched from the jaws of a famous French victory.

The upshot of Napoleon's and Gramont's instructions to Benedetti was the famous encounter between the ambassador and King William at Bad Ems on the morning of 13 July. Waylaying the monarch while he strolled in the Kürgarten, Benedetti persisted in raising the question of guarantees, despite William's obvious reluctance to discuss the issue. The exchange was courteous enough, but ended on a slightly abrupt note. Later in the day, William refused to grant the ambassador an audience, though he did send word to confirm that he had received official confirmation of the withdrawal of the candidature and that he considered the affair at an end. In the afternoon, he telegraphed an account of the day's proceedings to Bismarck, who was now back in Berlin, poised for action. By editing the sovereign's telegram, then making it public at home and abroad, Bismarck succeeded in conveying the impression that a huge snub had been administered to the French envoy. It was a calculated manoeuvre to goad the French into war, 'a red rag to the gallic bull'. It did not fail to produce the desired result.

Before the arrival of the news about the Ems telegram, Ollivier still hoped that peace could be preserved. Public opinion was dangerously inflamed, but his instincts were to try to cool the situation. At the council meeting held at Saint Cloud (around the same time that Benedetti was making his play to the Prussian king), Ollivier successfully insisted that the demand for guarantees should not be regarded as an ultimatum: even if William refused, the affair should be forgotten. The court did not take kindly to this decision. Nor was parliament prepared to let Ollivier and Gramont rest content with Leopold's renunciation, as they discovered from the storm of criticism they faced on the afternoon of 13 July. Nevertheless, on the morning of 14 July, while Ollivier was still planning a pacific statement for the chambers, Gramont arrived with word about the Ems telegram, describing it as 'a slap in the face'.[11] Ollivier himself recognised it as the dreaded *échec* which justified war.

Hastily, a council was convened at the Tuileries. The meeting began around 12.30 p.m. and went on for more than five hours. Gramont threatened to resign if war was not declared. Leboeuf pressed the case for immediate mobilisation and was given permission to go off to call up the reserves. Yet a number of ministers continued to plead for peace, especially since it was now known that Benedetti had not been the object of any deliberate insult on the part of the Prussian king. Ollivier offered to make a pacific declaration to the chambers, knowing that he would be defeated and replaced by a war ministry, but having thereby safeguarded the emperor from the charge that he was embarking on war for personal and dynastic reasons. Napoleon vetoed the suggestion and expressed his confidence in his ministers. As the afternoon wore on, no agreement could be reached on a form of words to be read to the parliamentarians. Eventually, consensus was found for the idea of a European congress. Napoleon seized upon it with tears in his eyes. Before leaving the Tuileries, he sent a missive to Lebœuf telling him that it was now less urgent to call up the reserves.[12]

At Saint Cloud, the war party was outraged. Lebœuf demanded another council to clarify what his orders were. Napoleon once again summoned his ministers, and this time they were less reluctant to contemplate war. Even Ollivier had reconsidered, rejecting the idea of a congress as both cowardly and chimerical. Like the Emperor, he claimed to be powerless before the force of public opinion.[13] The order to call up the reserves was maintained, though a formal decision to opt for war was postponed until another council held the following morning. The Empress attended both of the last two council meetings but remained silent. Napoleon applauded the statement prepared for the Legislative Body and the Senate by Ollivier and Gramont. In the end, the war was his as much as Bismarck's.

When Gramont read the declaration to the Senate on the afternoon of 15 July, it met with enthusiastic approval. Ollivier's reception in the Legislative Body was more mixed. The request for war credits of 50 million francs was opposed by a number of republican deputies and by Thiers. Above the din, the latter asked: 'Do you want all Europe to say that although the substance of the quarrel was settled, you have decided to pour out torrents of blood over a mere matter of form?' Ollivier replied that he accepted war '*d'un coeur léger*', with a light heart – an unfortunate choice of words which was to haunt him for the rest of his long life. Most deputies agreed with the one who bellowed: 'Prussia has forgotten the France of Jena and we must remind her.'[14] The credits were voted 245 to ten. War was not officially declared until 19 July. As Thiers – and Bismarck – had foreseen, in the eyes of the other powers France was the aggressor, and had to fight alone.

All of Napoleon's schemes for the enlistment of allies came to nothing. The south German states committed themselves to Prussia, in fulfilment of their alliance obligations. The great powers kept their distance. Austria-Hungary remembered 1866 and feared reactions. Italy wanted Rome, which Napoleon would not concede, out of deference to the French right. Britain, as always, had no desire to become entangled in the affairs of the Continent. Publication of Benedetti's draft treaty of 1866 in *The Times* on 25 July merely reinforced a position which had already been decided upon. Russia, long denied the revision of the Treaty of Paris which she wanted, and still sore about French attitudes during the Polish crisis, had every reason to see Prussia as a more useful ally than France. Indeed, most of the powers preferred to see a Prussian rather than a French victory. Prussia appeared to have a definite, but limited, objective in going to war – to complete the unification of Germany. Nobody could say with any precision what French war aims were – perhaps to establish a new era of French hegemony? The isolation of France was as much an indictment of Napoleon III's diplomatic failures as a tribute to Bismarck's finesse.

. . .

## WAR AND DEFEAT

Success in a war against Prussia would have guaranteed the indefinite survival of the Empire. It was widely anticipated. Had not Lebœuf given his assurances that the French army was ready 'down to the last gaiter button'? Were not French troops equipped with the *chassepot*, the most advanced rifle of its time? Some even had the *mitrailleuse*, the new machine gun. Napoleon himself was one of the few people with a sense of foreboding and an appreciation of France's true unprepared-ness. Nevertheless, there was no reason to believe that defeat was inevitable. The outcome was decided on the battlefields, where time and again the heroic endeavours of the French soldiers were nullified by the mind-boggling errors of the high command.

Napoleon was responsible for the worst mistake, his own appointment as commander-in-chief. Having designated the Empress as regent, he set off for the front on 28 July. Too ill to mount a horse, he went by train, and took his fourteen-year-old son with him. His first act was to change Lebœuf's organis-ational plans; instead of three armies, each headed by a mar-shal, there was to be only one single army, under himself, based at Metz. This order brought more confusion to a mobilisation which was already proceeding with less than exemplary effi-ciency. After two weeks, the army of the Rhine numbered only 200,000, not the 385,000 that Lebœuf had undertaken to raise. Officers wandered in search of their units. Supplies were as deficient as men; arms, uniforms, baggage-carts, ambulances, even maps, were lacking. The railway lines were clogged, impeding rather than facilitating the mobilisation.

To the amazement of the Prussians, the French were unable to carry the fight to their territory. A slight French success in a skirmish at Saarbrucken on 2 August was soon overtaken by three serious defeats in as many days when the Prussians launched their own attack in Alsace and Lorraine. On 4 August, a small French advance force under General Abel Douay was beaten at Wissembourg in Alsace, and its commander killed. On 6 August MacMahon was defeated at the battle of Froesch-willer and the way to Paris was opened up. A daring counter-offensive might still have turned the tide, as Moltke realised, but on 7 August, sitting in a railway carriage at Metz station, Napoleon heard how, the previous day, General Frossard had sustained another French defeat at Spicheren in Lorraine. He panicked, and ordered the whole army to retreat to the camp of Châlons. His health was giving way, his resolution had cracked and he had begun to resign himself to ultimate defeat.

News of the decision shocked the government in Paris: Ollivier cabled to say that it would have a disastrous effect on morale in the rear. Napoleon therefore changed the order to a retreat towards Metz, which created further confusion in the chain of command and fresh havoc in the provisioning of supplies. By this time, he was suffering agonies from the stone, and was willing to relinquish the supreme command and return to Paris, as Ollivier also desperately wanted. On 9 August, with considerable difficulty, he persuaded the Empress to summon him home, but under pressure from Ollivier's enemies on the right, who wanted to make the minister rather than the Emperor the scapegoat for the defeats, she changed her mind and told him to stay away. So Napoleon remained with the army, and committed the further error of handing command over to Bazaine, a man who possessed physical courage and had risen through the ranks, but had no relish for high responsibility. (Lebœuf would have been a better choice, but he, too, was being targeted by the politicians as a sacrificial victim.) It is true that Bazaine's authority was undermined by the continuing presence of the Emperor, now giving 'advice' rather than orders, which to Bazaine was the same thing.

The Empire was threatened, but not doomed, by the early reverses. Panic spread to Paris, where the republicans, having failed to prevent the outbreak of the war, took the lead in denouncing failure to prosecute it successfully. They demanded that the citizenry be armed for the defence of the capital. Fearing a *coup d'état*, Chevandier, the Minister of the Interior, favoured the arrest of the leading figures in the republican movement, including some twenty-two deputies. He was over-ruled by Ollivier, who was unwilling to act in so grave a matter without the Emperor by his side. It was for that reason that he urged Napoleon to return to the capital, only to be thwarted by the intrigues of his enemies. On 9 August, he discovered that he had lost the support of all groups in the Legislative Body, right, left and centre. Clément Duvernois, a leading right-wing Bonapartist, put a motion of no confidence, demanding a ministry 'capable of organising the defence of the country'. Only ten members supported Ollivier. He resigned, and was replaced by the comte de Palikao, the veteran of the Chinese expedition of 1860.

The overthrow of Ollivier brought the end of the Empire closer. Napoleon was effectively removed from power by his own followers, who, working through the Empress, repeatedly warned him to keep away from Paris and denied him the chance to master the political situation. Unable to impose his authority at home, and having renounced command of his troops, he was left in a kind of limbo. Yet while he remained with the troops Bazaine would undertake no initiative of his own. His plan was to retreat to Metz, where, after a fleeting French victory at Borny and another disastrous defeat at Gravelotte-Saint-Privat on 18 August, he found himself entrapped. Just in time, Napoleon had already taken himself off to the camp of Châlons, where he joined up with the remains of MacMahon's army, still a serviceable weapon of war.

On 17 August, his cousin Plon-Plon came to give him good advice. He insisted that it was still possible to prevent a total collapse, and to hold out indefinitely around Paris. The imperative need was for the Emperor to return to the capital and forestall revolution by appointing General Trochu, known for his liberal views and prescient criticisms of the army's weaknesses, as military governor. During this council of war, attended also by MacMahon, Trochu and other military chiefs, Napoleon sat listless and dejected. 'I seem to have abdicated,' he said pathetically.[5] A shadow of the man he had been, he would not engage in the energetic course of action urged upon him by his cousin, but obeyed the Empress's injunctions to stay away. He could not return without a victory, she said: otherwise there would be revolution on the streets of Paris.

Military logic was therefore subordinated to misguided political calculations, and MacMahon was ordered by the government to go to the relief of Bazaine. Full of doubts, he advanced ponderously towards Metz. Napoleon, in excruciating pain and with his face rouged to conceal the full extent of his illness, trailed behind, his presence not merely a hindrance to his generals but a provocation to the ordinary soldiers, who resented his train of baggage wagons and retinue of liveried servants.

The Germans cornered them at the fortress town of Sedan. The French gave battle on 1 September in response to an attack launched by Bavarian troops in the early hours. Outnumbered by more than two to one, and faced with overwhelmingly superior artillery, they stood no chance. MacMahon himself was wounded, and handed over command to General Ducrot, who tried to effect a further retreat to save at least a remnant of the army. He was overruled by General Wimpffen, a ferocious commander sent by Palikao to breathe fire into the troops and to obtain victory at any price. The slaughter was horrific. Napoleon rode out to where the fighting was heaviest, vainly courting death. Finally, unable to stomach the carnage any longer, he raised a white flag from the citadel of Sedan, to Wimpffen's fury. In a short letter to the King of Prussia he wrote, '*Monsieur mon frère*, having been unable to die at the head of my troops, it remains only for me to place my sword in the hands of your majesty'.[16] The Germans wanted a complete capitulation. On the morning of 2 September, Napoleon met with Bismarck, Moltke and William I and refused to negotiate peace terms, proclaiming himself a prisoner of war and no longer head of state. He did, however, authorise the surrender of the army of Châlons and its 84,000 men. In the afternoon he was given permission to telegraph the terrible news to Paris.

Unofficial, but reliable, word of the disaster reached the capital in the early evening of 2 September. Jérôme David broke the bad news to Eugénie and to members of the government. In the afternoon of 3 September, with rumours rife on the streets, Palikao was obliged to make a statement to the legislature. It signalled the end of the regime. The question which now preoccupied the deputies was purely one of form: could a transfer of power be arranged legally? The stumbling block was the Empress. On receiving Napoleon's own confirmation of the surrender, she had at first given vent to a fit of uncontrollable rage, cursing her husband's failure to die honourably on the battlefield, which alone might have won some sympathy for the succession of her son. Then, having pulled herself together, she resisted invitations to abdicate, insisting that it was her duty to stay at her post. In vain, Eugénie solicited the help of Thiers, then of Trochu, the military governor of Paris. While the government temporised, the more radical deputies became restless, and demanded a midnight sitting of the Legislative Body. Palikao confirmed that the Emperor was now a prisoner and, still playing for time, ajourned the session until midday on 4 September. As the debate on the transfer of power continued, it was rendered academic by the action of the crowd which, having poured into the streets of central Paris all morning, burst into the chamber and demanded the proclamation of the Republic. In time-honoured fashion, Favre, Gambetta and other republican deputies led the masses off to the Hôtel de Ville to proclaim the Republic. In the meantime, other sections of the crowd had begun an invasion of the Tuileries, precipitating the flight of Eugénie. The empire was over, even if the war was not.

. . .

## NOTES AND REFERENCES

1. *The Times*, 1 July 1870
2. Quoted by Zeldin T 1963 *Emile Ollivier and the Liberal Empire*. Clarendon Press, p. 174
3. Williams R 1971 *The Mortal Napoleon III*. Princeton University Press, p. 140
4. Steefel L 1962 *Bismarck, the Hohenzollern Candidacy, and the Origins of the Franco-German War of 1870*. Harvard University Press
5. Ibid., p. 115
6. Ibid., p. 122
7. Ibid., p. 133
8. These reactions are cited in ibid., p. 146; cf. Ollivier E *L'Empire libéral: études, récits, souvenirs*, vol 14, pp. 228–31
9. Steefel 1962, p. 149
10. Gall L 1986 *Bismarck: the White Revolutionary*, 2 vols, vol. 1, Allen & Unwin
11. Ollivier, vol. 14, p. 354
12. Steefel 1962, pp. 202–3 and 216–19
13. Ollivier, vol. 14, pp. 381–82
14. Howard M 1962 *The Franco-Prussian War: the German Invasion of France, 1870–1871*. Rupert Hart-Davis, p. 56
15. Ibid., p. 185
16. Ibid., p. 219

# EPILOGUE

After Sedan, Napoleon went to Germany as a prisoner and remained at the palace of Wilhelshöhe for six and a half months. He continued to live in monarchical style and received many visitors. The French press carried bitter denunciations of his comfortable situation as compared to the fate of ordinary prisoners-of-war, herded into Prussian camps. Because of the Provisional Government's refusal to cede Alsace Lorraine, the war dragged on until 29 January 1871, when, after the long and dreadful siege of Paris, the French finally capitulated and agreed to sign an armistice. Fresh elections were held for a new National Assembly. It met at Bordeaux on 1 March and, having blamed Napoleon III for all the disasters that had befallen the country, officially deposed him. Only six deputies dared to vote against the resolution.

Released from his Prussian captors, Napoleon made his way to England in March 1871 and established a new home with Eugénie and the Prince Imperial at Camden Place, Chiselhurst, a mansion with some twenty rooms, which accommodated approximately sixty friends, retainers and servants apart from the imperial family. Two days before he reached England, the Paris Commune was proclaimed, inaugurating yet another French civil war which culminated in the 'bloody week' of 21–28 May: after fearful atrocities committed by both sides, some 20,000 *communards* were slaughtered by soldiers acting ultimately under the authority of Thiers. This distinctly unpromising start to the new regime raised Bonapartist hopes of a restoration, and plans were even laid for another *coup d'état* to be carried out in March 1873. In exile, however, Napleon's health remained poor, and from the summer of 1872 he suffered so much from the stone that his English doctors advised a series of operations, which began in January 1873. The third, performed on 7 January, left him very weak, and on the morning of 9 January, at 10.45 a.m., before he could be operated upon again for a fourth time, he died. A post-mortem revealed that he had also been suffering from a kidney disease which would have killed him in a few years even had he survived the stone operation.

Since his death, Napoleon III has been reinvented many times: reviled by the republican 'black legend', branded a precursor of Hitler and Mussolini, and hailed as a 'modern' forerunner of European unity and Gaullist technocracy. The reinventions are instructive about the perspectives from which different historians have conducted their analysis, but they are inevitably misleading as attempts to place Napoleon in the context of his own times. The 'modern' Napoleon III, for instance, reflects the rise of economic history as a discipline and a twentieth-century infatuation with state-sponsored economic growth – and little else. In this book, Napoleon has been represented as an original in French politics, an unpredictable maverick who was at the same time a visionary and, above all, a highly skilled political operator. His 'profile in power' reveals that his advent to power, in the first instance, was fortuitous, a by-product of the introduction of manhood suffrage in 1848. In power, he rarely achieved precisely what he wanted, either at home or abroad. Many of his actions had consequences which he neither intended nor desired. The debate between his admirers and his detractors has become sterile. Both camps should remember that, perhaps more than most other rulers, Napoleon came to know all about the ironies of power.

# CHRONOLOGICAL TABLE

1808     Birth of Charles Louis Napoleon, future Napoleon III

1817     Hortense and Louis Napoleon established at Arenenberg (Switzerland) and Augsburg (Bavaria)

1831     Louis Napoleon and his brother Napoleon Louis participate in uprising in the Romagna (Papal State). Death of Napoleon Louis. Louis Napoleon and Hortense in Paris, then exiled to England

1832     *Rêveries Politiques*. Death of duc de Reichstadt (Napoleon II)

1833     *Political and Military Considerations on Switzerland*

1834     Captain of Artillery, Berne

1836     Abortive Strasbourg coup. Louis Napoleon exiled to America

1837     Death of Hortense

1838     Franco-Swiss conflict over residence of Louis Napoleon. Leaves for London

1840     Boulogne *putsch*. Imprisonment at Ham till 1846

1841     *Historical Fragments: 1688 and 1830*

1842     *Analysis of the Sugar Question*

1844     *On the Extinction of Pauperism*

1845     *On the Nicaragua Canal*

1846     Escape from Ham: back in London

1848    *April*: Special constable in London
*June*: Elected to National Assembly in by-elections: resigns
*September*: Re-elected. Returns to take his seat
*December*: Presidential elections. Louis Napoleon becomes President of the Second Republic

1849    Intervention against Roman Republic

1850    Falloux Law. Modification to Electoral Law. Repression of political activity

1851    *2 December: Coup d'état*. Plebiscite.

1852    *January*: New Constitution
*February*: Legislative elections
*September–October*: Tour of centre and south. Bordeaux speech
*November*: Restoration of Empire approved by plebiscite
*2 December*: Second Empire established

1853    Marriage to Eugénie

1854    Beginning of Crimean War

1855    Sebastopol taken. Paris Exhibition

1856    Treaty of Paris. Birth of Prince Imperial

1857    Legislative elections

1858    *January*: Orsini assassination attempt
*February*: Law of General Security
*July*: Plombières meeting with Cavour
*December*: Treaty with Piedmont

1859    War with Austria: Magenta and Solferino
Armistice of Villafranca. Treaty of Zurich

1860    Cobden–Chevalier Treaty of Commerce. Acquisition of Nice and Savoy. Syrian expedition. Palikao in China. 'Liberal' decrees

1861    Mexican expedition

1863    Polish crisis. Legislative elections

1864  Danish crisis. Labour reforms: law on 'coalitions' legalises strikes.
*15 September*: Convention with Italy, providing for withdrawal of French troops from Rome. Encyclical *Quanta Cura* and Syllabus of Errors.

1865  *Histoire de Jules César* (vol 2, 1866)
Paris–Biarritz talks with Bismarck

1866  Sadowa. Venetia ceded to Napoleon III, then to Italy. Last troops leave Rome

1867  More liberal reforms promised. Withdrawal of French from Mexico: execution of Maximilian. International Exhibition in Paris. Luxembourg crisis. Mentana and return of French troops to Rome.

1868  Niel Law – military reform blocked. Trade unions tolerated. Press liberalised

1869  Legislative elections. More reforms announced. Dismissal of Rouher. Suez Canal opened

1870  *January*: Ministry of Ollivier. Victor Noir Affair
*April*: New Constitution
*8 May*: Plebiscite
*July*: Hohenzollern crisis. War with Prussia
*1 September*: Sedan
*4 September*: Flight of Eugénie, fall of Empire, proclamation of Republic
Napoleon imprisoned at Wilhelmshöhe

1871  Armistice. Paris Commune.
*19 March*: Napoleon released; retires to Chiselhurst
*23 May*: Treaty of Frankfurt

1873  *9 January*: Death of Napoleon III

# BIBLIOGRAPHICAL ESSAY

All French titles are published in Pais unless otherwise stated.

## PRIMARY SOURCES

There is, sadly, no collected edition of the correspondence of Napoleon III. Many of his letters remain scattered through the diplomatic archives of Europe. Some are cited in translation by his official biographer B Jerrold 1874–82 *The Life of Napoleon III*, 4 vols, Longman. Almost 200 others are given in E de Hauterive 1925 *Napoléon III et le Prince Napoléon (Correspondance inédite)*, along with more than fifty replies. Some 300 are available in Napoleon III 1937 *Lettres de Napoléon III à Madame Cornu, en grande partie inédites. Texte intégral, publié et commenté par Marcel Emerit*, 2 vols. Some letters to Eugénie written in 1870 and 1871 may be found in *Revue des Deux Mondes* 1 September 1930. Printed collections containing correspondence of the Emperor include 1861– *Documents diplomatiques: Livres jaunes*; 1910–32 *Les origines diplomatiques de la Guerre de 1870–71*, 29 vols: 1926–29 *Il carteggio Cavour–Nigra 1858–61*, 4 vols: P Pirri (ed) 1944–45 *Pio IX e Vittorio Emmanuele II dal loro carteggio privato*, 3 vols; H Oncken (ed) 1926 *Die Rheinpolitik Kaiser Napoleon III, von 1863 bis 1870 und der Ursprung des Krieges von 1870/71: Nach den Staatsakten von Österreich, Preussen and den süddeutschen Mittelstaaten*, 3 vols; and G Bonnin (ed) 1957 *Bismarck and the Hohenzollern Candidature for the Spanish Throne: the Documents in the German Archives*.

Napoleon's own writings and speeches are obviously of major importance. See his 1869 *Oeuvres*, 5 vols and 1868 *La politique impériale exposée par les discours et proclamations de l'Empereur Napoléon III depuis le 10 décembre 1848 jusqu'en février 1868*. A shorter selection is made by R H Edleston (ed) 1931 *Napoleon III: Speeches from the Throne, together with Proclamations and Some Letters of the Emperor*, R I Severs. 1871 *Papiers et correspondance de la famille impériale*, 2 vols, contain material which the enemies of the Empire published with the aim of discrediting the regime.

Foreign ambassadors also recorded conversations with Napoleon III and their impressions of him. See, for instance, V Wellesley and R Sencourt 1934 *Conversations with Napoleon III*, Ernest Benn, which gives the recollections of British Ambassador (1852–67) Lord Cowley and J A von Hübner 1804 *Neuf ans de souvenirs d'un ambassadeur d'Autriche à Paris sous le Second Empire 1851–1859*, the memoirs of the Austrian ambassador. Also noteworthy are Baron E Beyens 1924–26 *Le Second Empire vu par un diplomate belge*, 2 vols; Lord Newton 1913 *Lord Lyons: a Record of British Diplomacy*, 2 vols; and the Third Earl of Malmesbury, 1885 *Memoirs of an Ex-Minister: an Autobiography*, 2 vols, Longman, Green. The memoirs of Napoleon's ministers also throw light on their master. Emile Ollivier's lengthy *apologia* is a fundamental, if flawed, source: see E Ollivier 1895–1918 *L'Empire libéral, études, récits, souvenirs*, 17 vols and 1 table. The same author's revealing *Journal 1846–1869*, 2 vols, has been edited by 1961 T Zeldin and Diaz A. Troisier de. Maupas C de 1884–85 *Mémoires sur le Second Empire*, 2 vols, is revealing on the *coup d'état*, as are duc de Morny 'La genèse d'un Coup d'Etat' *Revue des Deux Mondes* 1 December 1925 and Earl of Kerry (ed) 1924 *The Secret of the Coup d'Etat*, Constable. Napoleon's *fidus Achates* Persigny also published his memoirs: namely, F duc de Persigny 1896 *Mémoires du duc de Persigny publiés avec des documents inédits, un avant-propos et un épilogue*. So, too, did other servants and admirers of the Emperor: V Duruy 1901 *Notes et Souvenirs*, 2 vols; G Haussmann 1890–93 *Mémoires*; J L C A Randon 1875–77 *Mémoires du Maréchal Randon*, 2 vols; Maréchal de Castellane 1897 *Journal 1804–1862*, 5 vols; and General E comte de Fleury 1897–98 *Souvenirs du General Comte Fleury*. G Massa-Gille edited 1979 the *Journal d'Hippolyte Fortoul, ministre de l'Instruction Publique et des Cultes (1811–1856), vol I, 1er janvier-30 juin 1855*. Madame Jules Baroche 1921 *Second Empire: Notes et souvenirs de seize années (1855 à 1871)* is disappointingly thin. In addition to Victor Hugo, hostile contemporary witnesses include O Barrot 1876 *Mémoires posthumes*, 4 vols; Charles de Rémusat 1958–67 *Mémoires de ma vie*, 5 vols, (ed) C Pouthas; A Darimon 1883 *Histoire de douze ans (1857–1869)*; and T Delord

1867–75 *Histoire du Second Empire*, 6 vols. A source much used by Anglophone historians is N W Senior 1880 *Conversations with Distinguished Persons during the Second Empire*, 2 vols, Hurst & Blackett.

. . .

## SECONDARY SOURCES

Chapter 1 gives the essential historiographical outline: note 1 cites the most helpful bibliographies. Useful reference tools are 1987 *Historical Dictionary of France from the 1815 Restoration to the Second Empire*, 2 vols E L Newman (ed) and 1985 *Historical Dictionary of the French Second Empire 1852–1870* W E Echard (ed), both published by Greenwood Press.

Napoleon III has never lacked Anglophone biographers, many of them interested mainly in the more colourful aspects of his private life. In this genre J Ridley 1979 *Napoleon III and Eugénie*, Constable, is preferable to the more recent J Bierman 1989 *Napoleon III and His Carnival Empire*, John Murray. I Guest 1952 *Napoleon III in England*, British General & Technical Press, is likewise of anecdotal interest. Most of the biographies in English are favourable – notably those of Guerard, Corley and Smith (cited in the notes to Chapter 1) – though J M Thompson 1954 *Louis Napoleon and the Second Empire*, Blackwell, and J P T Bury 1964 *Napoleon III and the Second Empire*, English Universities Press, have their reservations.

The best modern French study is A Dansette *Histoire du Second Empire*, vol 1 1961, *Louis Napoléon à la conquete du pouvoir*, and vol 2 1972, *Du 2 décembre au 4 septembre*. Vol 3 1976 is significantly entitled *Naissance de la France moderne*. In the same vein see S Desternes and H Chandey 1961 *Napoléon III, homme du xxe siècle*. Napoleon's most recent French biographer, L Girard 1986 *Napoléon III*, remains critical, but is a long way removed from the abusive tradition of the 'black legend'. F A Simpson 1951 (3rd edn; 1st edn 1909) *The Rise of Louis Napoleon* is still the standard work on the early life of the Pretender, though he needs to be complemented by Dansette, vol 1. M Emerit 1937 *Madame Cornu et Napoléon III* is also worth consulting.

The wider context of the years spent in preparation for power is surveyed by R Magraw 1983 *France 1815–1914: the Bourgeois Century*, William Collins, and in more detail by A Jardin and A J Tudesq 1983 (original French edn 1973) *Restoration and Reaction*

*1815–1848*, Cambridge University Press, and H A C Massingham 1988 *The July Monarchy: a Political History of France 1830–1848*, Longman, all with extensive bibliographies. Also relevant are D Pinkney *The French Revolution of 1830*; D Johnson 1963 *Guizot: Aspects of French History 1781–1874*, Routledge & Kegan Paul; and the collected essays in J M Merriman (ed) *1830 in France*, New View Points and J M Merriman (ed) *Consciousness and Class Experience in Nineteenth Century Europe*, Holmes & Meier. B Fitzpatrick 1983 *Catholic Royalism in the Department of the Gard 1814–1852*, Cambridge University Press, is good on Legitimism, as are C H Johnson 1974 *Utopian Communism in France: Cabet and the Icarians, 1839–1851*, Cornell University Press and E Berenson 1984 *Populist Religion and Left-wing Politics in France 1830–1852*, Princeton University Press, on aspects of Utopian socialism.

The Bonapartist phenomenon is best approached via F Bluche 1980 *Le Bonapartisme: aux origines de la droite autoritaire (1800–1850)*, and, for popular Bonapartism, B Ménager 1988 *Les Napoléons du peuple*. The contemporary accounts of Marx and Tocqueville cited in the notes to Chapter 3 remain essential reading on 1848 and may be followed by M Agulhon 1983 (original French edn, 1973) *The Republican Experiment 1848–1852*, Cambridge University Press, and R Price 1972 *The French Second Republic*, Batsford. See also R Price (ed) 1975 *Revolution and Reaction: 1848 and the Second Republic*, Croom Helm. D McKay 1933 *The National Workshops*, Harvard University Press, still repays study.

On the June Days, consult G Rudé 1964 *The Crowd in History*, J. Wiley; F A de Luna 1969 *The French Republic under Cavaignac*, Princeton University Press; and M Traugott 1985 *Armies of the Poor: Determinants of Working-Class Participation in the Parisian Insurrection of June 1848*, Princeton University Press.

Louis Napoleon's reactions to these events can be gathered from P Duchon 'Les élections de 1848', *Revue de Paris* 15 March 1936, while the presidential election campaign is covered, with copious extracts from the contemporary press, by A J Tudesq 1965 *L'Election présidentielle de Louis-Napoléon Bonaparte 10 décembre 1848*.

Louis Napoleon as President of the Second Republic is a subject that still requires further research. Among the aspects which have been studied are the Falloux Law in R D Anderson 1975 *Education in France 1848–70*, Clarendon Press, and the

Roman expedition in the article by W E Echard 'Louis Napoleon and the French decision to intervene at Rome in 1849: a new appraisal', *Canadian Journal of History* IX (December 1974), pp. 263–74.

For the repressive aspects of the regime, see J Merriman 1978 *The Agony of the Republic: the Repression of the Left in Revolutionary France 1848–51*, Yale University Press.

Resistance to the *coup d'état* is impressively studied by T Margadant 1979 *French Peasants in Revolt: the Insurrection of 1851*, Princeton University Press.

The best short introduction to the history of the Empire is A Plessis 1985 (original French edn, 1979) *The Rise and Fall of the Second Empire 1852–1871*, Cambridge University Press, but it has little to say about foreign policy. P de la Gorce 1894–1904 *Histoire du Second Empire*, 7 vols, remains unsurpassed as a lengthy narrative account. How the 'official candidate' system worked – then ceased to work – is explained by T Zeldin 1958 *The Political System of Napoleon III*, Macmillan. The works of V Wright (see Chapter 5, notes 6 and 7) are important for the administrative system, as is L Girard, A Prost and R Gossez 1967 *Les Conseillers généraux en 1870: étude statistique d'un personnel politique*. H C Payne 1965 *The Police State of Louis Napoleon Bonaparte 1851–1860*, University of Washington Press, refutes the more fanciful 'proto-fascist' interpretations of the Second Empire, though the repressiveness of the general security law of 1858 is not to be underestimated. On this see V Wright 1969 'La loi de sûreté générale de 1858' *Revue d'Histoire Moderne et Contemporaine* (July–September).

Biographies of important ministers include R Schnerb 1949 *Rouher et le Second Empire*; J Maurain 1936 *Un bourgeois français au xixe siècle: Baroche, ministre de Napoléon III*; J Rohr 1967 *Victor Duruy, ministre de Napoléon III: essai sur la politique de l'instruction politique au temps de l'Empire libéral*, N Blayau 1969 *Billault, ministre de Napoléon III d'après ses papiers personnels, 1805–1863*; J M Chapman and B Chapman 1957 *The Life and Times of Baron Haussmann*, Weidenfeld & Nicolson: M Parturier 1969 *Morny et son temps*; H Farat 1957 *Persigny, un ministre de Napoléon III*; P Raphael and M Gontard 1976 *Un ministre de l'instruction publique sous l'Empire autoritaire: Hippolyte Fortoul (1851–1856)*.

The special case of Emile Ollivier is studied by T Zeldin 1963 *Emile Ollivier and the Liberal Empire*, Clarendon Press. The vital question of the Emperor's health is the subject of R Williams 1971 *The Mortal Napoleon III*, Princeton University Press.

The key work on relations between Church and state is J Maurain 1930 *La politique ecclésiastique du Second Empire de 1852 à 1869*. It can be supplemented with T Zeldin (ed) 1970 *Conflicts in French Society: Anticlericalism, Education and Morals in the Nineteenth Century*, Allen & Unwin, and A Gough 1986 *Paris and Rome: the Gallican Church and the Ultramontane Campaign 1848–1853*, Clarendon Press. M L Brown's biography of Louis Veuillot (Chapter 5, note 12) should be supplemented with *Louis Veuillot, Colloque de L'Institut Catholique de Paris* in *Revue de l'Institut Catholique de Paris*, 10 (April–June 1884) and J Gadille 1964 'Autour de Louis Veuillot et de l'Univers', *Cahiers d'Histoire*. The general situation of French Catholics may be appreciated in G Cholvy and Y M Hilaire 1985 *Histoire religieuse de la France contemporaine*, vol 1, 1800–1880, and R Gibson 1989 *A Social History of French Catholicism 1789–1914*, Routledge. R P Lecanuet 1895–1902 *Montalembert*, 3 vols, is still the major work on the leading light of French liberal Catholicism, though a more general treatment of the phenomenon is 1974 *Les Catholiques libéraux au xixe siècle Colloque de Grenoble 1971*. J Gadille 1969 *Albert du Boÿs, ses 'souvenirs du concile du Vatican, 1869–1870': l'intervention du gouvernement impérial à Vatican I* is illuminating on the French government's attitude to the Vatican Council.

There is no recent study in English of the republican opposition to the Second Empire, though S Elwitt 1975 *The Making of the Third Republic: Class and Politics in France 1868–1884*, Louisiana State University Press, contains some insights. Even in French one has to turn to older works like G Weill 1928 *Histoire du parti républicain (1814–1870)* and I Tchernoff 1960 *Le Parti républicain au coup d'état et sous le Second Empire*, though these may now be supplemented with impressive regional studies such as B Ménager 1983 *La vie politique dans le département du Nord de 1851 à 1877*, 3 vols, and R Huard 1982 *Le mouvement républicain en Bas-Languedoc, 1848–81*. On the elections of 1869 there is L Girard (ed) 1960 *Les élections de 1869*. Biographies shed some light on the situation. On Blanqui there is M Dommanget 1960 *Blanqui et l'opposition républicaine à la fin du Second Empire* and on Rochefort, R Williams 1966 *Henri Rochefort, Prince of the Gutter Press*, Scribners.

The definitive work on Napoleon III's foreign policy has still to be written, but the starting point for research must now be the extremely full bibliography listed in W E Echard 1988 *Foreign Policy of the Second Empire: a Bibliography*, Greenwood Press. Two surveys are P Renouvin 1940 *La politique extérieure du Second Empire*, mimeograph cours de Sorbonne, and A Pignaud 1927 'La politique extérieure du Second Empire', *Revue Historique* CLV (September–October). The general context of international relations is given by P Renouvin 1954 in P Renouvin (ed) *Histoire des relations internationales*, vol 5, *Le xixe siècle I: De 1815 à 1871* and A J P Taylor 1954 *The Struggle for Mastery in Europe 1848–1918*, Clarendon Press. W E Mosse 1958 *The European Powers and the German Question, 1848–1871: with Special Reference to England and Russia*, Cambridge University Press, has archival-based material on aspects of Napoleon's policy. P Henry 1943 *Napoléon III et les peuples: à propos d'un aspect de la politique extérieure du Second Empire* is justifiably sceptical about the Emperor's commitment to any pure *politique des nationalités*. W E Echard 1983 *Napoleon III and the Concert of Europe*, Louisiana State University, is the most valuable recent work, even if it tends to press its (revisionist) thesis too hard. L Case 1954 *French Opinion on War and Diplomacy during the Second Empire*, University of Pennsylvania Press, was a path-breaking study of the role of public opinion in the formulation of French foreign policy. In the same connection, see also N Isser 1974 *The Second Empire and the Press: a Study of Government-inspired Brochures on French Foreign Policy in their Propaganda Milieu*, Martinus Nijhoff. N N Barker 1968 *Distaff Diplomacy: the Empress Eugénie and the Foreign Policy of the Second Empire*, University of Texas Press, dispels the myths about the evil influence of the Empress over her husband in the matter of foreign policy.

As regards particular episodes, the phase of the Crimean War may be approached via B D Gooch 1956, 'A century of historiography on the origins of the Crimean War', *American Historical Review* LXII (October), pp. 33–58, and A Ramm 1960 'The Crimean War' in *New Cambridge Modern History*, Vol X, *The Zenith of European Power 1830–1870*.

The literature on Napoleon III and Italy is enormous, if inconclusive. Italian perspectives on Plombières and the Italian war may be obtained from D Mack Smith 1985 *Cavour*, Weidenfeld & Nicolson; R Romeo 1984 *Cavour e il suo tempo vol 3 1854–1861*, and F Valsecchi 1961 'L'unificazione italiana e la politica europea (1849–1859)', in *Nuove Questioni di Storia del*

*Risorgimento e dell'Unità d'Italia*, vol 1, pp. 721–64. Also relevant is E E Y Hales 1954 *Pio Nono: a Study in European Politics and Religion in the Nineteenth Century*, Eyre & Spottiswoode. On the Roman question, see I Scott 1969 *The Roman Question and the Powers 1848–1865*, Martinus Nijhoff, and N Blakiston (ed) 1962 *The Roman Question: Despatches of Lord Odo Russell 1858–1870*, Chapman & Hall.

Some of the threads of French policy are unravelled by F C de Bernardy 1976 'Alexandre Walewski et la question italienne', *Revue d'Histoire Diplomatique* 90 (July–December), pp. 245–64; L M Case 1976 *Edouard Thouvenel et la diplomatie du Second Empire*; and L M Case 1932 *Franco-Italian Relations 1860–1865: the Roman Question and the Convention of September*, University of Pennsylvania Press.

The important issue of Venetia has been studied by J W Bush 1967 *Venetia Redeemed: Franco-Italian Relations 1864–1866*, University of Syracuse Press, and N N Barker 1964 'Austria, France and the Venetian question, 1861–1866', *Journal of Modern History* XXXVI, pp. 145–54. Still useful is C W Hallberg 1955 *Franz Joseph and Napoleon III 1852–1864: a Study of Austro-French Relations*, Octagon.

An alternative assessment of the Biarritz conversations to that presented here is P Bernstein 1971 'Napoleon III and Bismarck: the Biarritz–Paris talks of 1865', in N N Barker and M L Brown (eds) *Diplomacy in an Age of Nationalism: Essays in Honor of Lynn Marshall Case*, Martinus Nijhoff, pp. 124–43.

The best guide to Franco-Prussian relations is E A Pottinger 1966 *Napoleon III and the German Crisis 1865–1866*, Harvard University Press, though also valuable is W A Fletcher 1965 *The Mission of Vincent Benedetti to Berlin, 1864–1870*, Martinus Nijhoff.

The final crisis is ably reconstructed by L Steefel 1962 *Bismarck, the Hohenzollern Candidacy, and the Origins of the Franco-German War of 1870*, Harvard University Press. The short-comings of the army are revealed by R Holmes 1984 *The Road to Sedan: the French Army 1866–1870*, Royal Historical Society, and the *débâcle* described by M Howard 1962 *The Franco-Prussian War: the German Invasion of France, 1870–1871*, Rupert Hart-Davis.

The 'modern' aspects of the Second Empire have been the subject of much recent research, particularly in economic history. Part One of R Price 1987 *A Social History of Nineteenth Century France*, Hutchinson, deals with the evolution of the economy and gives an up-to-date bibliography. On the commercial treaty of 1860, A Dunham 1930 *The Anglo-French Treaty of Commerce of 1860*, University of Michigan Press, has been superseded by B M Ratcliffe 1975 'Napoleon III and the Anglo-French Commercial Treaty of 1860: a reconsideration', in B M Ratcliffe (ed) *Great Britain and Her World 1750–1914*, Manchester University Press. L Girard 1951 *La politique des travaux publics du Second Empire* was a landmark in the historiography. D Pinkney 1958 *Napoleon III and the Rebuilding of Paris*, Princeton University Press, can still be read with profit, though a fuller study of the transformation of Paris is now the thesis of J Gaillard 1977 *Paris, la ville (1852–1870)*.

On the social policy of the Emperor there are D Kulstein 1969 *Napoleon III and the Working Class: a Study of Government Propaganda under the Second Empire*, California State Colleges, and H N Boon 1936 *Rêve et réalité dans l'oeuvre de Napoléon III*, Martinus Nijhoff. G Boilet 1961 *La doctrine sociale de Napoléon III* is the work of a fanatical Bonapartist rather than a serious study of Napoleon's ideas. For the conditions of working-class life, G Duveau 1946 *La vie ouvrière en France sous le Second Empire* is still required reading, as is P Pierrard 1965 *La vie ouvrière à Lille sous le Second Empire*. Y Lequin 1977 *La formation de la classe ouvrière régionale: les ouvriers de la région lyonnaise (1848–1914)*, 2 vols, is a major thesis, while W H Sewell Jr 1974 'Social change and the rise of working-class politics in nineteenth-century Marseille', *Past and Present* 65, pp. 75–109 is suggestive.

Industrial strife is analysed in F L'Huillier 1957 *La lutte ouvrière à la fin du Second Empire*. T Judt 'The French labour movement in the nineteenth century', in T Judt 1986 *Marxism and the French Left*, Clarendon Press, underlines the importance of the Empire in the evolution of the labour movement.

The colonial history of the period is under-researched, but a beginning may be made with J Marseille 1985 'The phases of French colonial imperialism: towards a new periodisation', *Journal of Imperial and Commonwealth History* 13, pp. 127–41, and, for Algeria, C A Julien 1964 *Histoire de l'Algérie contemporaine*, vol 1.

The Mexican misadventure has generated a large literature. N N Barker 1979 *The French Experience in Mexico 1821–1861: a History of Constant Misunderstanding*, University of North Carolina Press, gives the background. E E C Corti 1927 *Maximilien et Charlotte du Mexique*, 2 vols (translated from the German), contains many original letters. C Scheffer 1939 *La grande pensée de*

*Napoléon III: les origines de l'expédition du Mexique, 1858–1862* sees Saint-Simonian influences at work, while monetary aspects are emphasised by S Black 1978 'Napoléon III et le Mexique: un triomphe monétaire', *Revue Historique* CCLIX, pp. 55–73. G Martinière 1974 'L'expédition mexicaine de Napoléon III dans l'historiographie française', *Revue d'Histoire Moderne et Contemporaine* XXI (January–March) is a good guide to the various interpretations of Napoleon's motives.

# MAPS

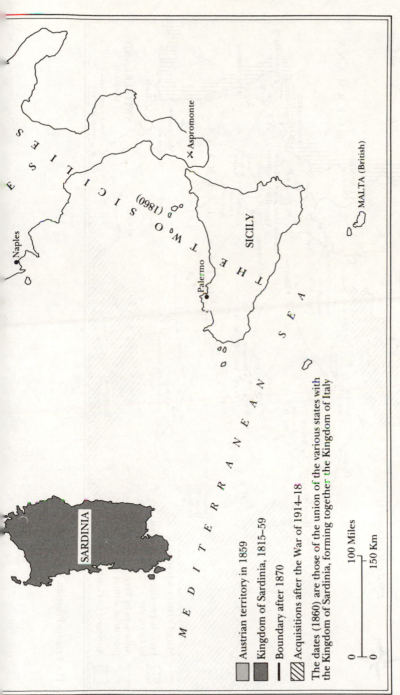

Austrian territory in 1859

Kingdom of Sardinia, 1815–59

Boundary after 1870

Acquisitions after the War of 1914–18

The dates (1860) are those of the union of the various states with the Kingdom of Sardinia, forming together the Kingdom of Italy

0 — 100 Miles
0 — 150 Km

I. Italian Unification

MEDITERRANEAN SEA

SARDINIA

THE TWO SICILIES

SICILY

Palermo

X Aspromonte

Naples

MALTA (British)

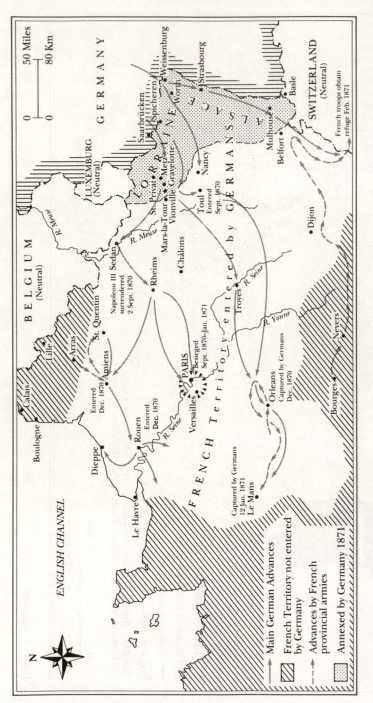

2. The Franco-Prussian War, 1870–1

3. The Departments of France (shown for the purpose of electoral geography)

# INDEX